Y0-CXS-937

FABLES IN SLANG *AND* MORE FABLES IN SLANG

FABLES IN SLANG *AND* MORE FABLES IN SLANG

by George Ade

Illustrations by Clyde J. Newman
With an Introduction by E. F. Bleiler

DOVER PUBLICATIONS, INC.
NEW YORK, NEW YORK

Copyright © 1960 by Dover Publications, Inc.

All rights reserved under Pan American and
International Copyright Conventions.

Published simultaneously in Canada by
McClelland and Stewart Limited.

Published in the United Kingdom by
Constable and Company Limited
10 Orange Street, London, W.C. 2.

This new Dover edition, first published in 1960 is
a republication of *Fables in Slang* and *More Fables*
as published by Herbert S. Stone and Company
in 1899 and 1900. Illustrations for this edition
were selected from the original editions and a new
Introduction was written for this edition by E. F.
Bleiler.

This edition was designed by Geoffrey K. Mawby

Manufactured in the United States of America

Dover Publications, Inc.
180 Varick Street
New York 14, New York

INTRODUCTION *TO* DOVER EDITION

GEORGE ADE

G EORGE ADE (1866-1944) was one of the most gifted of the many creative writers who worked on American newspapers around 1900. A tall thin man who used to complain about his resemblance to Woodrow Wilson, he had emerged from a small town in Indiana, where his father had been at various times blacksmith, bank cashier, and small farmer. George was one of a large family, and when it was discovered that he was too fond of reading and thinking to be trusted with the cows, he was sent to the newly founded Purdue University.

After graduating from Purdue, George Ade made his first contribution to American culture while working in the advertising department of a drug manufacturer: he coined the trade name "Cascarets." This job ended after a time, however, and several jobs later Ade found himself on the staff of the *Chicago News-Record* (later the *Record*) as a cub reporter.

Ade and the newspaper agreed. Ade was bright, conscientious, affable, and had the power of words. Within a few years he had worked up through the levels of reporting fires, the police court, and local sports to being a star reporter and the man the *Record* sent to cover the really important events. An Ade interview or an Ade coverage usually meant increased readership.

One of Ade's duties on the *Record* was to fill two columns in each issue with a feature called "Stories of the Streets and of the Town." This feature was based upon the daily life of Chicago, and from 1893 to 1900, when Ade left the *Record,* it was one of the treasures of the newspaper world. While Ade may have had peers in general writing ability, no one else had his keen eye or his ability to saturate stories with personal charm. It was in his column, in September 1897, that the first "fable in slang" appeared.

Let Ade himself describe its creation, as quoted by Fred Kelly in *George Ade, Warmhearted Satirist:*

> I sat at the desk and gazed at the empty soft paper, and realized the necessity of concocting something different. The

changes had been wrung . . . on blank verse, catechisms, rhyme, broken prose, the drama form of dialogue, and staccato paragraphs. Why not a fable for a change? And instead of slavishly copying Aesop and LaFontaine, why not retain the archaic form and the stilted manner of composition, and for purposes of novelty, permit the language to be 'fly,' modern, and undignified, quite up to the moment.

The result, which appeared on September 17, 1897, was entitled "This Is a Fable." It made use of slang and colloquial expressions, intermingled with standard English, but it differed from the later fables in having all words hyphenated according to syllables. It is reprinted here, in revised form, as "The Fable of Sister Mae, who Did as Well as Could Be Expected."

"This Is a Fable" was popular, but it caused no great outburst of enthusiasm. It was not until two years later, in July 1899, that the next slang fables appeared, now frankly labelled "Fables in Slang." These are the fables printed here, slightly revised, as "The Fable of the Slim Girl Who Tried to Keep a Date that was Never Made" and "The Fable of the New York Person who Gave the Stage Fright to Fostoria, Ohio."

Ade's publisher, Herbert S. Stone of Chicago, now stepped in. Stone, who had already published three books built up from Ade's column (*Artie, Pink Marsh,* and *Doc' Horne*), had had Ade under contract for quite a while to do a novel; all Ade's friends expected it to be the Great American Novel. It was entitled *The College Widow,* and presumably had the same plot as Ade's later play of the same name. Beautifully bound dummy copies of the novel were carried around by Stone's salesman, and advance sales had been rather good. The only difficulty was that Ade did not deliver the manuscript. He said he had no time.

Stone agreed to take a series of fables instead of *The College Widow* and from July through October 1899 "Stories of the Streets and of the Town" was often filled with new slang sketches. In October 1899 the first edition of *Fables in Slang* appeared. It met with remarkable success, selling almost 70,000 copies within a year. The *Record* started to syndicate some of the fables to other newspapers, and Ade was suddenly surprised to learn that he had become wealthy and financially independent. *More Fables* appeared in October 1900. Some of its sketches had appeared in the *Record* and other newspapers, but more than half of its contents had never appeared elsewhere. It, too, was a great success. George Ade now found himself a national figure, and his slang fable, which had begun as a day's stop-gap, was recognized as a new art and humor form.

II

Fables in Slang is slightly awry as a title, since the sketches are technically not fables, and the slang element in them is small. They are really written in the vernacular, in the colloquial tradition of Josh Billings, Bill Nye, and "Mr. Dooley." Yet Ade had contributed something new to American literature, for never before had the fable flourished in America. Hawthorne, it is true, had written a few allegorical fables, and Bierce had written a whole series of bitter fables; but Hawthorne was too occasional, and Bierce was too ferocious and too abstract to be a successful fabulist. Ade, on the other hand, succeeded spectacularly, and critics as well as readers acclaimed his work. Ade had worried a little about professional literary critics, since he was using vernacular English, but even the representatives of the Brahmin tradition liked the fables: Brander Matthews praised them highly, and W. D. Howells called them "almost absolute in perfection." Mark Twain, H. L. Mencken, and Carl Sandburg were also among Ade's most enthusiastic admirers.

With *Fables in Slang* Ade had now become the eye for the American reading public. He made visible the hitherto unseen people who made up America: the inhabitants of the boarding house and the farm town, the small stage performers, the college students, politicians, working men, and merchants. He pointed out their habits, and showed how quaint and unusual were the things that everyone had seen for years, but had not perceived. Ade spread color over the drab and trivial, and anyone who read one of his books received a very pleasant exercise in perception and analysis.

Ade was also the American heart. He had the unmatched gift of making readers laugh at situations and plots that would have been depressing (or boring) if they had been written by Zola or Frank Norris or any turn-of-the-century naturalistic writer. His subject matter, surprisingly enough for a topical humorist, is often tragic. Try retelling, in your own words, one of Ade's better fables, and you will probably be surprised at the depths of pessimism, despair, and frustration that it really conceals. You will find yourself talking about misfits who lose all hope, mental weaklings who shatter themselves against their misconceptions, and limited people who are trapped in situations far beyond them. Try restating the fable of the Slim Girl or of Paducah's Favorite Comedians, and you will discover, as you finish, that you have told a very sad story.

Yet so great was Ade's skill with the *mot juste,* the proper authorial wink and nudge, the right bit of flippancy, that hundreds of thousands of readers laughed at his work. By stripping a tragic situation of its individuality, making it a type, compressing it to its bare essentials, and covering it with a closely fashioned cocoon of wit, Ade broke the power of the bitterness which his fables concealed. Yet despite the fact that Ade wrote humorously about unhappiness, he was not a mocker. He was not mildly cynical like his great predecessors in the 18th century, nor was he ferociously cynical like Bierce. He was really a very warm-hearted man who had great compassion for the prototypes of his stories.

Ade's fables have no common theme, and the "morals" at their end are often flippant and irreverent. Ade, as a rule, was not a preacher, and he neither attacked nor defended morals; he remained aloof from questions of right and wrong. For Ade, life was tragic, and good intentions did not mitigate pain; morality does not always pay, nor does immorality, either. This is a universe of irrelevancies and randomness, and it doesn't matter much what you do as long as you mind your own business.

The ideas that emerge from the fables, apart from the underlying pessimism and frustration, are meagre. Ade was not a systematic thinker, and was not greatly interested in ideas. Nor did he have any messianic misunderstandings about himself. H. L. Mencken, who admired him as a craftsman, once called him a "parade-goer" and a "boor with a touch of genius." It must be admitted that Mencken was not too far wrong, if you interpret "boor" to mean "provincial" (as Mencken seems to have meant it), instead of "ill-bred." The fables abound in xenophobia, and Ade is always suspicious of "culture" or any other values than those which might appeal to the readers of the *Chicago Record*. You can find his spiritual descendants in syndicated newspaper cartoonists. Like his contemporaries in humor, however, Ade loathed hypocrisy, and a considerable portion of the fables is devoted to pricking those who suffer from self-inflation.

Today the fables have an additional value as interesting period pieces. They offer a remarkably faithful microcosm of life in Chicago and the Middle West in the last part of the 19th century. Although they are often written with humor of exaggeration and they seldom give specific description, they are saturated with the folk-psychology of their day. Their period slang is no bar to comprehension. Although an Englishman may have found them difficult when they first appeared some sixty years ago, Ade's fables should now be intelligible to almost anyone in the English-speaking world. It is a tribute to his insight that his slang, where it has not survived, is readily understandable from context.

III

Fables in Slang and *More Fables* were reprinted many times. In 1914 Ade adapted them to a series of films for the Essanay Film Company, and in the 1920's he rewrote many of them for newspaper publication. In 1927 the fables were syndicated as comic strips with drawings by Art Helfant.

Ade continued to write fables in slang, and altogether wrote ten volumes of them, containing more than two hundred and fifty different fables: *Fables in Slang* (1899); *More Fables* (1900); *Forty Modern Fables* (1901); *The Girl Proposition* (1902); *People You Know* (1903); *Breaking Into Society* (1904); *True Bills* (1904); *Knocking the Neighbors* (1912); *Ade's Fables* (1914); and *Hand-Made Fables* (1920). He also wrote more than two hundred and fifty uncollected fables which appeared in such magazines as Hearst's *International* and *Cosmopolitan* and have never been reprinted.

Ade wrote easily, usually a fable at a sitting; he made few alterations from his first drafts. He seldom had to think hard to find subjects, for his was the fortunate ability to create character at a moment's notice. His slang he picked up as he heard it, and he was careful to state in his later life that he had never used thieves' cant or the jargon of the racetrack, but had used only phrases that could be read with propriety in any family. At first he wrote by ear, and his slang was small in quantity. Like many another author who was known by a mannerism, however, he was gradually forced to increase the amount of slang as he wrote new fables, so that the fables of the 1920's are far different from those of the carefree *Chicago Record* days. These later fables are often in the manner of George Ade, rather than George Ade. Ade disliked his fables (much as Conan Doyle came to dislike the Sherlock Holmes stories), and would groan at each new assignment; but at one dollar a word he managed to find paper and ideas.

What ever became of *The College Widow* and the Great American Novel that Ade's friends were sure he could write? After 1900 Ade was a wealthy man, and could write very much what he wanted to write: this did not include novels. Instead, he turned to the area that had always meant most to him, in both private life and writing—the popular stage. Ade had always been stage-struck; the first color that came into his drab boyhood had been from the stage, and he never outgrew his delight for anything that happened behind footlights. As Ade himself admitted, his critical faculty became suspended when he entered a theatre.

Ade's facility and deftness brought him a second fortune from work that was unworthy of the fabulist. He peopled scores of stages, both circuit and Broadway, with potboilers like *The Sultan of Sulu* and *The College Widow,* now as a play. But Ade was no playwright and his plays are as ephemeral as his fables are long-lived. It is sad to compare the early fable of the two mandolin players with the dramatic version of it that Ade sold to *The Country Gentleman* in 1928.

Ade's later life, after the first series of fables, was uneventful. He wrote many plays, most of which made money. He also did a few movie scenarios. He wrote occasional newspaper essays, short stories, and poems, few of which are now read or remembered. He traveled around the world several times, collected rents from his empire of farms in Indiana, took part in politics (Bull Moose and Republican), and entertained his friends sumptuously. In short, he enjoyed himself.

He seems to have been a remarkable amiable man, charming to everyone he met, once a slight initial shyness wore off. It has been said, in all seriousness, that no one ever saw him angry. Wealth and important friends never turned his head. He was on close friendly terms with literally hundreds of people who lived near his estate in Indiana, and his gigantic banquets, to which everyone for miles around would be invited, are still remembered. He was generous to a fault. It was discovered at his death in 1944 that he had been supporting not only some of his old friends, but many people who were complete strangers, and had simply appealed to him for help.

Ade never married. He used to say that the only woman he ever loved had married another man. This romance, which occurred in his college years, had died when the girl's family objected to Ade's lack of religion, and Ade had become discouraged. Other women never seem to have attracted him, even though as a playwright he was on friendly terms with the most beautiful actresses of his day. His essay on the blessings of bachelorhood has been called one of the saddest writings in American literature.

Today Ade has achieved a strange sort of fame. He is represented by a fable or two (or occasionally a short story) in practically every collection of American humor, yet at the time this introduction is being written, not one of his books is in print. Perhaps this long-deserved reissue of his earliest collections of fables* will bring him the evaluation that he merits, away from both the frantic adulation that met his hack stage work and the complete neglect that he has fallen into. His fables, I am sure, deserve recognition. They are remarkably perceptive, often brilliantly written, and are still funny and pertinent to the American scene.

As for George Ade himself, I imagine that he will be listed among those who had talent but wasted it; as a peculiarly limited genius; as a man who could do many things easily, but often put superior work into an inferior product.

---

* One fable in *More Fables* has been omitted from this edition: "The Fable of the Man-Grabber Who Went Out of His Class." To modern readers this fable is offensive. Standards of taste have changed greatly since it was written, especially with regard to minority groups, and we are sure that Ade himself would now agree that this fable could well be omitted.

Some modern writer should write a fable about Ade himself. It would be simple in treatment. An earnest, very gifted young man goes to the big city to make his fortune. He works hard, and becomes wealthy in a very short time; but instead of continuing to use his resources, as everyone had expected, he retires, to enjoy himself. The Moral: Don't Expect your Friends to Write the Great American Novel Simply because they Have Intelligence and Leisure.

New York, 1960   **E. F. BLEILER**

TABLE *OF* CONTENTS

TABLE *OF* CONTENTS

FABLES
IN SLANG

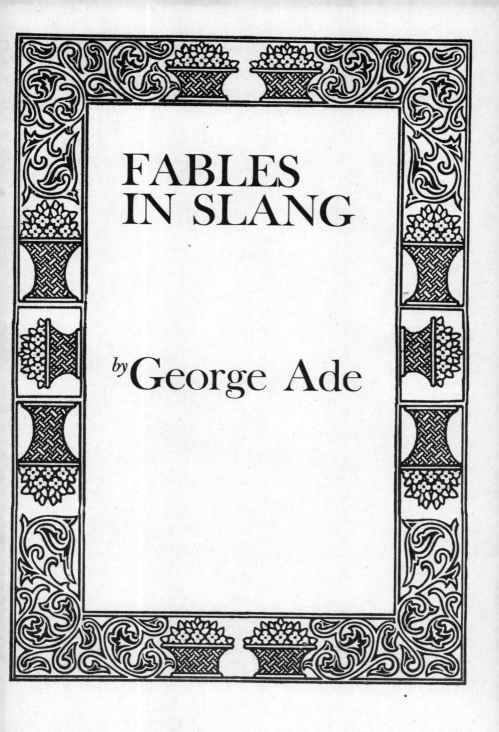

FABLES IN SLANG

by George Ade

THE FABLE OF THE VISITOR WHO GOT
A LOT FOR THREE DOLLARS

THE Learned Phrenologist sat in his Office surrounded by his Whiskers.

Now and then he put a Forefinger to his Brow and glanced at the Mirror to make sure that he still resembled William Cullen Bryant.

Near him, on a Table, was a Pallid Head made of Plaster-of-Paris and stickily ornamented with small Labels. On the wall was a Chart showing that the Orangoutang does not have Daniel Webster's facial angle.

"Is the Graft played out?" asked the Learned Phrenologist, as he waited. "Is Science up against it or What?"

Then he heard the fall of Heavy Feet and resumed his Imitation. The Door opened and there came into the Room a tall, rangy Person with a Head in the shape of a Rocky Ford Cantaloupe.

Aroused from his Meditation, the Learned Phrenologist looked up at the Stranger as through a Glass, darkly, and pointed to a Red Plush Chair.

The Easy Mark collapsed into the Boarding-House Chair and the Man with more Whiskers than Darwin ever saw stood behind Him and ran his Fingers over his Head, Tarantula-Wise.

"Well, well!" said the Learned Phrenologist. "Enough Benevolence here to do a family of Eight. Courage? I guess yes! Dewey's got the same kind of a Lump right over the Left Ear. Love of Home and Friends—like the ridge behind a Bunker! Firmness—out of sight! Reverence—well, when it comes to Reverence, you're certainly There with the Goods! Conscientiousness, Hope, and Ideality—the Limit! And as for Metaphysical Penetration—of, Say, the Metaphysical Penetration, right where you part the Hair—oh, Laura! Say, you've got Charles Eliot Norton whipped to a Custard. I've got my Hand on it now. You can feel it yourself, can't you?"

"I can feel Something," replied the Human Being, with a rapt Smile.

"Wit, Compassion and Poetic Talent —right here where I've got my Thumb—a C inch! I think you'll run as high as 98 per cent on all the Intellectual Faculties. In your Case we have a Rare Combination of Executive Ability, or the Power to Command, and those Qualities of Benevolence and Ideality which contribute to the fostering of Permanent Religious Sentiment. I don't know what your present Occupation is, but you ought to be President of a Theological Seminary. Kindly slip me Three Dollars before you Pass Out."

THE LEARNED PHRENOLOGIST

The Tall Man separated himself from Two Days' Pay and then went out on the Street and pushed People off the Sidewalk, He thought so well of Himself.

Thereafter, as before, he drove a Truck, but he was always glad to know that he could have been President of a Theological Seminary.

MORAL: *A good Jolly is worth Whatever you Pay for it.*

HUMAN BEING

THE FABLE OF THE SLIM GIRL WHO TRIED TO KEEP A DATE THAT WAS NEVER MADE

ONCE upon a Time there was a slim Girl with a Forehead which was Shiny and Protuberant, like a Bartlett Pear. When asked to put Something in an Autograph Album she invariably wrote the Following, in a tall, dislocated Back-Hand:

"Life is Real; Life is Earnest,
And the Grave is not its Goal."

That's the kind of a Girl she was.

In her own Town she had the Name of being a Cold Proposition, but that was because the Primitive Yokels of a One-Night Stand could not Attune Themselves to the Views of one who was troubled with Ideals. Her Soul Panted for the Higher Life.

Alas, the Rube Town in which she Hung Forth was given over to Croquet, Mush and Milk Sociables, a lodge of Elks and two married Preachers who doctored for the Tonsilitis. So what could the Poor Girl do?

In all the Country around there was not a Man who came up to her Plans and Specifications for a Husband. Neither was there any Man who had any time for Her. So she led a lonely Life, dreaming of the One—the Ideal. He was a big and pensive Literary Man, wearing a Prince Albert coat, a neat Derby Hat and godlike Whiskers. When He came he would enfold Her in his Arms and whisper Emerson's Essays to her.

But the Party failed to show up.

Often enough she put on her Chip Hat and her Black Lisle Gloves and Sauntered down to look at the Gang sitting in front of the Occidental Hotel, hoping that the Real Thing would be there. But she always saw the same old line of Four-Flush Drummers from Chicago and St. Louis, smoking Horrid Cigars and talking about the Percentages of the League Teams.

She knew that these Gross Creatures were not prone to chase mere Intellectual Splendor, so she made no effort to Flag them.

When she was Thirty-Four years of age and was able to recite

4

"Lucile" without looking at the Book she was Married to a Janitor of the name of Ernest. He had been kicked in the Head by a Mule when young and believed everything he read in the Sunday Papers. His pay was Twenty-Three a month, which was high, if you knew Ernest.

COLD PROPOSITION

His Wife wore a red Mother Hubbard all during the Remainder of her Life.

This is invariably a Sign of Blasted Hopes.

MORAL: *Never Live in a Jay Town.*

FOUR-FLUSH DRUMMER

THE FABLE OF THE NEW YORK PERSON WHO GAVE THE STAGE FRIGHT TO FOSTORIA, OHIO

A NEW YORK man went to visit a Cousin in the Far West. The name of the Town was Fostoria, Ohio.

When he came into Town he had his Watch-Chain on the outside of his Coat, and his Pink Spats were the first ever seen in Fostoria.

"Have you a Manicure Parlor in this Beastly Hole?" asked the New York Man, as they walked up from the Train.

"What's that?" asked the Cousin, stepping on his own Feet.

"Great Heavens!" exclaimed the New York Man, and was silent for several Moments.

At Dinner he called for Artichokes, and when told that there were none, he said, "Oh, very well," in a Tone of Chastened Resignation.

After Dinner he took the Family into the Parlor, and told the Members how much they would Enjoy going to Weber and Fields'. Seeing a Book on the Table, he sauntered up to It and said, "Ah, one of Dick Davis' Things." Later in the Evening he visited the only Club House in Town. The Local Editor of the Evening Paper was playing Pin-Pool with the Superintendent of the Trolley Line. When the New York Man came into the Room, they began to Tremble and fell down on their Shots.

The Manager of the Hub and Spoke Factory then asked the New York Man to have a Drink. The New York Man wondered if a Small Bottle was already cold. They said Yes, but it was a Lie. The Boy had to go out for it.

He found One that had been in the Window of the Turf Exchange since the Grand Opening, the Year after Natural Gas was discovered. The New York Man drank it, remarking that it was hardly as Dry as he usually got it at Martin's.

The Club Members looked at Him and said Nothing. They thought he meant Bradley-Martin's.

Next Day the New York Man was Interviewed by the Local

7

Editor. He said the West had a Great Future. In the Evening he attended the Annual Dinner of the Bicycle Club, and went Home early because the Man sitting next to him put Ice in his Claret.

In due time he returned to New York, and Fostoria took off its White Shirt.

Some Weeks after that, the Cousin of the New York Man had

NEW YORK MAN

an Opportunity to visit the Metropolis. He rode on an Extra Ticket with a Stockman who was shipping three Car-Load of Horses, and got a Free Ticket for every Car-Load.

When the Cousin arrived at New York he went to the address, and found the New York Man at Dinner.

There was a Sheaf of Celery on the Table.

SNAKE CHARMER

Opposite the New York Man sat a Chiropodist who drank.

At his right was a Large Woman in a Flowered Wrapper—she had been Weeping.

At his left was a Snake-Charmer from Huber's Museum.

The New York Man asked the Cousin to wait Outside, and then explained that he was stopping there Temporarily. That Evening they went to Proctor's, and stood during the Performance.

MORAL: *A New York Man never begins to Cut Ice until he is west of Rahway.*

THE FABLE OF THE BASE BALL FAN WHO TOOK THE ONLY KNOWN CURE

ONCE upon a Time a Base Ball Fan lay on his Death-Bed. He had been a Rooter from the days of Underhand Pitching.

It was simply Pie for him to tell in what year Anse began to play with the Rockfords and what Kelly's Batting Average was the Year he sold for Ten Thousand.

If you asked him who played Center for Boston in 1886 he could tell you quick—right off the Reel. And he was a walking Directory of all the Glass Arms in the Universe.

More than once he had let drive with a Pop Bottle at the Umpire and then yelled "Robber" until his Pipes gave out. For many Summers he would come Home, one Evening after Another, with his Collar melted, and tell his Wife that the Giants made the Colts look like a lot of Colonial Dames playing Bean Bag in a Weedy Lot back of an Orphan Asylum, and they ought to put a Trained Nurse on Third, and the Dummy at Right needed an Automobile, and the New Man couldn't jump out of a Boat and hit the Water, and the Short-Stop wouldn't be able to pick up a Ball if it was handed to him on a Platter with Water Cress around it, and the Easy One to Third that ought to have been Sponge Cake was fielded like a One-Legged Man with St. Vitus dance trying to do the Nashville Salute.

Of course she never knew what he was Talking about, but she put up with it, Year after Year, mixing Throat Gargle for him and reading the Games to him when he was having his Eyes tested and had to wear a Green Shade.

At last he came to his Ninth Inning and there were Two Strikes called and no Balls, and his Friends knew it was All Day with him. They stood around and tried to forget that he was a Fan. His Wife wept softly and consoled herself with the Thought that possibly he would have amounted to Something if there had been no National Game. She forgave Everything and pleaded for one Final Message. His Lips moved. She leaned over and Listened.

He wanted to know if there was Anything in the Morning Papers about the Condition of Bill Lange's Knee.

MORAL: *There is a Specific Bacillus for every Classified Disease.*

THE FAN

THE FABLE OF THE GOOD FAIRY WITH THE LORGNETTE, AND WHY SHE GOT IT GOOD

O NCE Upon a Time there was a Broad Girl who had nothing else to do and no Children to look after, so she thought she would be Benevolent.

She had scared all the Red Corpuscles out of the 2 by 4 Midget who rotated about her in a Limited Orbit and was known by Courtesy as her Husband. He was Soft for her, and so she got it Mapped out with Herself that she was a Superior Woman.

She knew that when she switched the Current on to herself she Used up about 6,000 Ohms an hour, and the whole Neighborhood had to put on Blinders.

She had read about nine Subscription Books with Cupid and Dove Tail-Pieces and she believed that she could get away with any Topic that was batted up to her and then slam it over to Second in time to head off the Runner.

Her clothes were full of Pin-Holes where she had been hanging Medals on Herself, and she used to go in a Hand-Ball Court every Day and throw up Bouquets, letting them bounce back and hit Her.

Also, She would square off in front of a Camera every Two Weeks, and the Man was Next, for he always removed the Mole when he was touching up the Negative. In the Photograph the Broad Girl resembled Pauline Hall, but outside of the Photograph, and take it in the Morning when she showed up on the Level, she looked like a Street just before they put on the Asphalt.

But never you Fear, She thought She had Julia Arthur and Mary Mannering Seventeen up and One to play, so far as Good Looks were concerned; and when it came to the Gray Matter— the Cerebrum, the Cerebellum, and the Medulla Oblongata— May Wright Sewall was back of the Flag and Pulled up Lame.

The Down-Trodden Man, whom she had dragged to the Altar, sized Her all right, but he was afraid of his Life. He wasn't Strong enough to push Her in front of a Cable Car, and he didn't have the Nerve to get a Divorce. So he stood for Everything; but

in the Summer, when She skated off into the Woods to hear a man with a Black Alpaca Coat lecture to the High Foreheads about the Subverted Ego, he used to go out with a few Friends and tell them his Troubles and weep into his Beer. They would slap him on the Back and tell him she was a Nice Woman; but he knew better.

Annyhow, as Bobby Gaylor used to say, she became restless around the House, with nothing to do except her Husband, so she made up her mind to be Benevolent to beat the Band. She decided that she would allow the Glory of her Presence to burst upon the Poor and the Uncultured. It would be a Big Help to the Poor and Uncultured to see what a Real Razmataz Lady was like.

She didn't Propose to put on Old Clothes, and go and live with Poor People, and be One of Them, and nurse their Sick, as they do in Settlements. Not on Your Previous Existence! She was going to be Benevolent, and be Dead Swell at the Same Time.

Accordingly, she would Lace Herself until she was the shape of a Bass Viol, and put on her Tailor-Made, and the Hat that made her Face seem longer, and then she would Gallop forth to do Things to the Poor. She always carried a 99-cent Lorgnette in one Hand and a Smelling-Bottle in the Other.

"Now," she would say, feeling Behind to make sure that she was all strung up, "Now, to carry Sunshine into the Lowly Places."

As soon as she struck the Plank Walks, and began stalking her prey, the small Children would crawl under the Beds, while Mother would dry her Arms on the Apron, and murmur, "Glory be!" They knew how to stand off the Rent-Man and the Dog-Catcher; but when 235 pounds of Sunshine came wafting up the Street, they felt that they were up against a New Game.

The Benevolent Lady would go into a House numbered 1135A with a Marking Brush, and after she had sized up the front room through the Lorgnette, she would say: "My Good Woman, does your Husband drink?"

"Oh, yes, sir," the grateful Woman would reply. "That is, when he's working. He gets a Dollar Ten."

"And what does he do with all his Money?" the Benevolent Lady would ask.

"I think he plays the Stock Market," would be the Reply.

Then the Benevolent Lady would say: "When the Unfortunate Man comes Home this Evening you tell him that a Kind and Beautiful Lady called and asked him please to stop Drinking, except a Glass of Claret at Dinner, and to be sure and read Eight or Ten Pages from the *Encyclopædia Britannica* each Night before retiring; also tell him to be sure and save his Money. Is that your Child under the Bed?"

"That's little William J."

THE MIDGET

"How Many have you?"

"Eight or Nine—I forget Which."

"Be sure and dress them in Sanitary Underwear; you can get it for Four Dollars a Suit. Will you be good enough to have the Little Boy come from under the Bed, and spell 'Ibex' for the Sweet Lady?"

"He's afraid of you."

"Kindly explain to him that I take an Interest in him, even though he is the Offspring of an Obscure and Ignorant Workingman, while I am probably the Grandest Thing that ever Swept up the Boulevard. I must go now, but I will Return. Next time I come I hope to hear that your Husband has stopped Drinking and is very Happy. Tell the Small Person under the Bed that if he learns to spell 'Ibex' by the time I call again I will let him look at my Rings. As for you, bear in mind that it is no Disgrace to be Poor; it is simply Inconvenient, that's all."

Having delivered herself of these Helpful Remarks she would Duck, and the Uplifted Mother would put a Nickel in the Can and send Lizzie over to the Dutchman's.

In this manner the Benevolent Lady carried forward the Good Work, and Dazzled the whole Region between O'Hara's Box Factory and the City Dump. It didn't Cost anything, and she derived much Joy from the Knowledge that Hundreds of People were Rubbering at her, and remarking in Choked Whispers: "Say, ain't she the Smooth Article?"

But one day a Scrappy Kid, whose Mother didn't have any Lorgnette or Diamond Ear-Bobs, spotted the Benevolent Lady. The Benevolent Lady had been in the House telling his Mother that it was a Glorious Privilege to wash for a Living.

After the Benevolent Lady went away the Kid's Mother sat down and had a Good Cry, and the Scrappy Kid thought it was up to him. He went out to the Alley and found a Tomato Can that was not working, and he waited.

In a little while the Benevolent Lady came out of a Basement, in which she had been telling a Polish Family to look at her and be Happy. The Scrappy Kid let drive, and the Tomato Can struck the Benevolent Lady between the Shoulder Blades. She squawked and started to run, fell over a Garbage Box, and had to be picked up by a Policeman.

She went Home in a Cab, and told her Husband that the Liquor League had tried to Assassinate her, because she was Reforming so many Drunkards. That settled it with her—she said she wouldn't try to be Benevolent any more—so she joined an Ibsen Club.

The Scrappy Kid grew up to be a Corrupt Alderman, and gave his Mother plenty of Good Clothes, which she was always afraid to wear.

MORAL: *In uplifting, get underneath.*

THE BROAD GIRL

THE FABLE OF THE KID WHO SHIFTED HIS IDEAL

AN A. D. T. Kid carrying a Death Message marked "Rush" stopped in front of a Show Window containing a Picture of James J. Jeffries and began to weep bitterly.

A kind-hearted Suburbanite happened to be passing along on his Way to the 5.42 Train. He was carrying a Dog Collar, a Sickle, a Basket of Egg Plums and a Bicycle Tire.

The Suburbanite saw the A. D. T. Kid in Tears and it struck him that here was a Bully Chance to act out the Kind-Hearted Pedestrian who is always played up strong in the Sunday School Stories about Ralph and Edgar.

"Why do you weep?" he asked, peering at the Boy through his concavo-convex Nose Glasses.

"Oh, gee! I was just Thinking," replied the Urchin, brokenly. "I was just Thinking what chance have I got to grow up and be the Main Stem, like Mr. Jeffries."

"What a perverted Ambition!" exclaimed the Suburbanite. "Why do you set up Mr. Jeffries as an Ideal? Why do you not strive to be like Me? Is it not worth a Life of Endeavor to command the Love and Respect of a Moral Settlement on the Outskirts? All the Conductors on our Division speak pleasantly to Me, and the Gateman has come to know my Name. Last year I had my Half-Tone in the Village Weekly for the mere Cost of the Engraving. When we opened Locust avenue from the Cemetery west to Alexander's Dairy, was I not a Member of the Committee appointed to present the Petition to the Councilmen? That's what I was! For Six Years I have been a Member of the League of American Wheelmen and now I am a Candidate for Director of our new four-hole Golf Club. Also I play Whist on the Train with a Man who once lived in the same House with T. DeWitt Talmage."

Hearing these words the A. D. T. Kid ceased weeping and cheerfully proceeded up an Alley, where he played "Wood Tag."

MORAL: *As the Twig is Bent the Tree is Inclined.*

18

THE KID

THE FABLE *OF THE* UNINTENTIONAL
HEROES *OF* CENTREVILLE

IN Centreville there lived two husky Young Fellows named Bill and Schuyler—commonly abbreviated to Schuy. They did not find any nourishing Excitement in a Grain Elevator, so they Enlisted to Free Cuba.

The Government gave each of them a Slouch Hat and a pre-historic Firearm. They tied Red Handkerchiefs around their Necks and started for the Front, each with his Head out of the Car Window. They gave the Sioux Yell to everybody along the Track between Centreville and Tampa.

While in Camp they played Double Pedie, smoked Corn-Cob Pipes, and cussed the Rations. They referred to the President of these United States as "Mac", and spoke of the beloved Secretary of War as "Old Alger."

After more or less Delay they went aboard a Boat, and were landed in Cuba, where they began to Shoot at everything that looked Foreign. The hot Rain drenched them, and the tropical Sun steamed them; they had Mud on their clothes, and had to sleep out. When they were unusually Tired and Hungry, they would sing Coon Songs and Roast the War Department.

At last they were ordered Home. On the way back they didn't think of Anything except their two Lady Friends, who worked in the Centreville Steam Laundry.

They rode into Town with a Machete under each Arm, and their Pockets full of Mauser Cartridges.

The first Thing they saw when they alighted from the Train was a Brass Band. It began to play, "See the Conquering Hero Comes."

Then eight Little Girls in White began to strew Flowers in their Pathway.

The Artillery company ripped out a Salute.

Cap Gibbs, who won his Title by owning the first Steam Thrashing Machine ever seen in the County, confronted them with a Red, White, and Blue Sash around him. He Barked in a loud Voice —it was something about Old Glory.

Afterwards the Daughters of the Revolution took them in Tow, and escorted them to Pythian Hall, where they were given Fried Chicken, Veal Loaf, Deviled Eggs, Crullers, Preserved Water-melon, Cottage Cheese, Sweet Pickles, Grape Jelly, Soda Biscuit, Stuffed Mangoes, Lemonade, Hickory-Nut Cake, Cookies, Cinnamon Roll, Lemon Pie, Ham, Macaroons, New York Ice Cream, Apple Butter, Charlotte Russe, Peppermint Wafers, and Coffee.

SCHUY

While they were Feeding, the Sons of Veterans Quartet stood on the Rostrum with their Heads together, and sang:

> "Ten-ting to-night! Ten-ting to-night,
> Ten-ting on the old-ah Camp-ground!"

At the first opportunity Bill motioned to Schuyler, and led him into the Anteroom, where they kept the Regalia, the Kindling Wood, and the Mop.

"Say, Schuy, what the Sam Hill does this mean?" he asked; "are we Heroes?"

"That's what Everybody says."

"Do you Believe it?"

"No matter what I Believe; I'm goin' to let 'em have their own Way. I may want to Run for Supervisor some Day."

MORAL: *If it is your Play to be a Hero, don't Renig.*

THE FABLE OF THE PARENTS WHO TINKERED WITH THE OFFSPRING

A MARRIED Couple possessed two Boys named Joseph and Clarence. Joseph was much the older. His Parents brought him up on a Plan of their Own. They would not permit him to play with other Boys for fear that he would soil himself, and learn to be Rude and Boisterous.

So they kept Him in the House, and his Mother read to him about Little Rollo, who never lied or cheated, and who grew up to be a Bank President. She seemed to think that a Bank President was above Reproach.

Little Joseph was kept away from the Public Schools, and had to Play Games in the Garret with two Spindly Little Girls. He learned Tatting and the Herring-Bone Stitch. When he was Ten Years of age he could play Chop-Sticks on the Piano; his Ears were Translucent, and his Front Teeth showed like those of a Gray Squirrel.

The other Boys used to make Faces at him over the Back Fence and call him "Sis."

In Due Time he went to College, where he proved to be a Lobster. The Boys held him under the Pump the first Night. When he walked across the Campus, they would whistle, "I don't Want to Play in Your Yard." He began to drink Manhattan Cocktails, and he smoked Hemp Cigarettes until he was Dotty. One Day he ran away with a Girl who waited on the Table at his Boarding House, and his Parents Cast him Off. At Present he has charge of the Cloak Room at a Dairy Lunch.

Seeing that the Home Training Experiment had been a Failure in the case of Joseph, the Parents decided to give Clarence a large Measure of Liberty, that he might become Acquainted with the Snares and Temptations of the World while he was Young, and thus be Prepared to side-step the Pitfalls when he was Older. They sent him to the Public Schools; they allowed him to roam at large with other Kids, and stay out at Nights; they kept Liquor on the Sideboard.

Clarence stood in with the Toughest Push in Town, and thus became acquainted with the Snares and Temptations of the World. He learned to Chew Tobacco and Spit through his Teeth, shoot Craps and Rush the Can.

When his Father suggested that he enter some Business House,

JOSEPH

and become a Credit to the Family, he growled like a Boston
Terrier, and told his Father to go Chase Himself.

At present, he is working the Shells with a Circus.

MORAL: *It all depends.*

CLARENCE

THE FABLE *OF* HOW *HE* NEVER TOUCHED GEORGE

A COMIC Lover named George was sitting on the Front Porch with a good Side Hold on your old friend Mabel. They were looking into each other's Eyes at Close Range and using a rancid Line of Nursery Talk.

It was the kind of Conversation calculated to Jar a Person.

George murmured that Mabel was George's own Baby-Daby and she Allowed that he was a Tooney-Wooney Ittle Bad Boy to hold his Itsy-Bitsy Bun of a Mabel so tight she could hardly breave. It was a sort of Dialogue that Susan B. Anthony would love to sit up Nights to Read.

While they were Clinched, Mabel's Father, a large, Self-Made Man, came down the Stairway and out to the Veranda.

This is where the Fable begins to Differentiate.

Although the Girl's name was Mabel and the Young Man's name was George, and the Father was a Self-Made Man, the Father did *not* Kick the Young Man.

He asked him if he had Anything to Smoke.

George gave him an Imported Panetella and said He didn't believe it was going to Rain. Mabel's Father said it looked Black in the West, but he Reckoned it might blow around, like as not. Mabel said she wouldn't be a bit Surprised if it did blow around.

Mabel's Father told Mabel she could show George where the Ice-Box wuz in case he Expressed a Hankerin', and then he went down street to examine some Fishing Tackle just purchased by a Friend of his in the Hay and Feed Business. Just as Father struck the Cement Walk George changed to the Strangle Hold.

MORAL: *The Exception proves the Rule.*

MABEL'S FATHER

THE FABLE OF THE PREACHER WHO FLEW HIS KITE, BUT NOT BECAUSE HE WISHED TO DO SO

A CERTAIN Preacher became wise to the Fact that he was not making a Hit with his Congregation. The Parishioners did not seem inclined to seek him out after Services and tell him he was a Pansy. He suspected that they were Rapping him on the Quiet.

The Preacher knew there must be something wrong with his Talk. He had been trying to Expound in a clear and straightforward Manner, omitting Foreign Quotations, setting up for illustration of his Points such Historical Characters as were familiar to his Hearers, putting the stubby Old English words ahead of the Latin, and rather flying low along the Intellectual Plane of the Aggregation that chipped in to pay his Salary.

But the Pew-Holders were not tickled. They could Understand everything he said, and they began to think he was Common.

So he studied the Situation and decided that if he wanted to Win them and make everybody believe he was a Nobby and Boss Minister he would have to hand out a little Guff. He fixed it up Good and Plenty.

On the following Sunday Morning he got up in the Lookout and read a Text that didn't mean anything, read from either Direction, and then he sized up his Flock with a Dreamy Eye and said: "We cannot more adequately voice the Poetry and Mysticism of our Text than in those familiar Lines of the great Icelandic Poet, Ikon Navrojk:

"To hold is not to have—
Under the seared Firmament,
Where Chaos sweeps, and Vast Futurity
Sneers at these puny Aspirations—
There is the full Reprisal."

When the Preacher concluded this Extract from the Well-Known Icelandic Poet he paused and looked downward, breathing heavily through his Nose, like Camille in the Third Act.

A Stout Woman in the Front Row put on her Eye-Glasses and leaned forward so as not to miss Anything. A Venerable Harness Dealer over at the Right nodded his Head solemnly. He seemed to recognize the Quotation. Members of the Congregation glanced at one another as if to say: "This is certainly Hot Stuff!"

The Preacher wiped his Brow and said he had no Doubt that every one within the Sound of his Voice remembered what Quarolius had said, following the same Line of Thought. It was

GUFF

Quarolius who disputed the Contention of the great Persian Theologian Ramtazuk, that the Soul in its reaching out after the Unknowable was guided by the Spiritual Genesis of Motive rather than by mere Impulse of Mentality. The Preacher didn't know what all This meant, and he didn't care, but you can rest easy that the Pew-Holders were On in a minute. He talked it off in just the Way that Cyrano talks when he gets Roxane so Dizzy that she nearly falls off the Piazza.

The Parishioners bit their Lower Lips and hungered for more

GOOD AND PLENTY

First-Class Language. They had paid their Money for Tall Talk and were prepared to solve any and all Styles of Delivery. They held on to the Cushions and seemed to be having a Nice Time.

The Preacher quoted copiously from the Great Poet Amebius. He recited 18 lines of Greek and then said: "How true this is!" And not a Parishioner batted an Eye.

It was Amebius whose Immortal Lines he recited in order to prove the Extreme Error of the Position assumed in the Controversy by the Famous Italian, Polenta.

VENERABLE HARNESS DEALER

He had them Going, and there wasn't a Thing to it. When he would get tired of faking Philosophy he would quote from a Celebrated Poet of Ecuador or Tasmania or some other Seaport Town. Compared with this Verse, all of which was of the same School as the Icelandic Masterpiece, the most obscure and clouded Passage in Robert Browning was like a Plate-Glass Front in a State Street Candy Store just after the Colored Boy gets through using the Chamois.

After that he became Eloquent, and began to get rid of long Boston Words that hadn't been used before that Season. He grabbed a rhetorical Roman Candle in each Hand and you couldn't see him for the Sparks.

After which he sunk his Voice to a Whisper and talked about the Birds and the Flowers. Then, although there was no Cue for him to Weep, he shed a few real Tears. And there wasn't a dry Glove in the Church.

After he sat down he could tell by the Scared Look of the People in Front that he had made a Ten-Strike.

Did they give him the Joyous Palm that Day? Sure!

The Stout Lady could not control her Feelings when she told how much the Sermon had helped her. The venerable Harness Dealer said he wished to indorse the Able and Scholarly Criticism of Polenta.

In fact, every one said the Sermon was Superfine and Dandy. The only thing that worried the Congregation was the Fear that if it wished to retain such a Whale it might have to Boost his Salary.

In the Meantime the Preacher waited for some one to come and ask about Polenta, Amebius, Ramtazuk, Quarolius and the great Icelandic Poet, Navrojk. But no one had the Face to step up and confess his Ignorance of these Celebrities. The Pew-Holders didn't even admit among themselves that the Preacher had rung in some New Ones. They stood Pat, and merely said it was an Elegant Sermon.

Perceiving that they would stand for Anything, the Preacher knew what to do after that.

MORAL: *Give the People what they Think they want.*

THE JOYOUS PALM

THE FABLE *OF* HANDSOME JETHRO, *WHO WAS* SIMPLY CUT OUT *TO* BE *A* MERCHANT

AN Illinois Squab came home from Business College with a Zebra Collar and a pair of Tan Shoes big enough for a Coal Miner. When he alighted from the depot one of Ezry Folloson's Dray Horses fell over, stricken with the Cramp Colic. The usual Drove of Prominent Citizens who had come down to see that the Train got in and out all right backed away from the Educated Youth and Chewed their Tobacco in Shame and Abashment. They knew that they did not belong on the same Platform with One who had been up yender in Chicago for goin' on Twelve weeks finding out how to be a Business Man. By Heck!

An elderly Man approached the Youth who had lately got next to the Rules of Commerce. The elderly Man was a Yap. He wore a Hickory Shirt, a discouraged Straw Hat, a pair of Barn-Door Pants clinging to one lonely Gallus and woolen Socks that had settled down over his Plow Shoes. He was shy several Teeth and on his Chin was a Tassel shaped like a Whisk-Broom. If you had thrown a Pebble into this Clump of Whiskers probably you would have scared up a Field Mouse and a couple of Meadow Larks.

"Home agin, Jethro, be ye?" asked the Parent.

"Yeh," replied the Educated Youth. With that he pulled the Corner of a Sassy Silk Handkerchief out of his upper Coat Pocket and ignited a Cigarette that smelt like Burning Leaves in the Fall.

The Business Man went Home, and the Parent followed at a Respectful Distance, now and then remarking to Himself: "Well, I'll jest swan to Guinney!"

Brother Lyford came in from the East Eighty to get his Dinner, and there was Jethro in the Hammock reading a Great Work by Archibald Clavering Gunter.

"Git into some Overhauls an' come an' he'p Me this Afternoon," said Lyford.

"Oh, rats! Not on your Tintype! I'm too strong to work,"

replied Jethro, who had learned Oodles of slang up in Chicago, don't you forget it.

So he wouldn't Stand for the Harvest Field that afternoon. In the Evening when Paw ast him to Milk he let out an Awful Beller. Next Morning he made a Horrible Beef because he couldn't get Loaf Sugar for his Coffee.

Shortly after Breakfast his Paw lured him into the Barn and Lit on him. He got a good Holt on the Adam's Apple and choked the Offspring until his Tongue stuck out like a Pistil.

JETHRO

"You dosh-burned little Pin-Head o' Misery, you!" exclaimed
the Old Man. "Goll bing me if I think you're wuth the Powder
to.blow you up. You peel them Duds an' git to Work or.else
mosey right off o' this Farm."

The Son's Feelings were so outraged by this Brutal Treatment
that he left the Farm that Day and accepted a position in a Five
and Ten-Cent Store, selling Kitchen Utensils that were made of
Tin-Foil and Wooden Ware that had been painted in Water
Colors. He felt that he was particularly adapted for a Business
Career, and, anyway, he didn't propose to go out on No Man's
Farm and sweat down his Collar.

After Ten Years of Unremitting Application and Studious
Frugality the Business Man had acquired in Real Estate, Personal
Property, Stocks, Bonds, Negotiable Paper, and other Collateral,
the sum of Nineteen Dollars, but he owed a good deal more than
that. Brother Lyford had continued to be a rude and unlettered
Country Jake. He had 240 acres of crackin' Corn Land (all tiled),
a big red Barn, four Span of good Horses, sixteen Head of Cattle,
a likely bunch of Shoats and a Covered Buggy.

MORAL: *Drink Deep, or Cut Out the Pierian Spring Altogether.*

PAW

THE FABLE OF PADUCAH'S FAVOURITE COMEDIANS AND THE MILDEWED STUNT

ONCE Upon a Time there was a Specialty Team doing Seventeen Minutes. The Props used in the Act included a Hatchet, a Brick, a Seltzer Bottle, two inflated Bladders and a Slap-Stick. The Name of the Team was Zoroaster and Zendavesta.

These two Troupers began their Professional Career with a Road Circus, working on Canvas in the Morning, and then doing a Refined Knockabout in the Grand Concert or After-piece taking place in the Main Arena immediately after the big Show is over.

When each of them could Kick Himself in the Eye and Slattery had pickled his Face so that Stebbins could walk on it, they decided that they were too good to show under a Round Top, so they became Artists. They wanted a Swell Name for the Team, so the Side-Show Announcer, who was something of a Kidder and had attended a Unitarian College, gave them Zoroaster and Zendavesta. They were Stuck on it, and had a Job Printer do some Cards for them.

By utilizing two of Pat Rooney's Songs and stealing a few Gags, they put together Seventeen Minutes and began to play Dates and Combinations.

Zoroaster bought a Cane with a Silver Dog's Head on it, and Zendavesta had a Watch Charm that pulled the Buttonholes out of his Vest.

After every Show, as soon as they Washed Up, they went and stood in front of the Theater, so as to give the Hired Girls a Treat, or else they stood around in the Sawdust and told their Fellow-Workers in the Realm of Dramatic Art how they killed 'em in Decatur and had 'em hollerin' in Lowell, Mass., and got every Hand in the House at St. Paul. Occasionally they would put a Card in the Clipper, saying that they were the Best in the Business, Bar None, and Good Dressers on and off the Stage. Regards to Leonzo Brothers. Charley Diamond please write.

They didn't have to study no New Gags or work up no more Business, becuz they had the Best Act on Earth to begin with. Lillian Russell was jealous of them and they used to know Francis Wilson when he done a Song and Dance.

They had a Scrap Book with a Clipping from a Paducah Paper, which said that they were better than Nat Goodwin. When some

ZOROASTER

Critic who had been bought up by Rival Artists wrote that Zoro-aster and Zendavesta ought to be on an Ice Wagon instead of on the Stage, they would get out the Scrap Book and read that Paducah Notice and be thankful that all Critics wasn't Cheap Knockers and that there was one Paper Guy in the United States that reckanized a Neat Turn when he seen it.

But Zoroaster and Zendavesta didn't know that the Dramatic Editor of the Paducah Paper went to a Burgoo Picnic the Day the Actors came to Town, and didn't get back until Midnight, so he wrote his Notice of the Night Owls' performance from a Pro-gramme brought to him by the Head Usher at the Opera House, who was also Galley Boy at the Office.

Zoroaster and Zendavesta played the same Sketch for Seventeen Years and made only two important Changes in all that Time. During the Seventh Season Zoroaster changed his Whiskers from Green to Blue. At the beginning of the Fourteenth Year of the Act they bought a new Slap-Stick and put a Card in the Clipper warning the Public to beware of Imitators.

All during the Seventeen Years Zoroaster and Zendavesta continued to walk Chesty and tell People how Good they were. They never could Understand why the Public stood for Mansfield when it could get Zoroaster and Zendavesta. The Property Man gave it as his Opinion that Mansfield conned the Critics. Zenda-vesta said there was only one Critic on the Square, and he was at Paducah.

When the Vodeville Craze came along Zoroaster and Zenda-vesta took their Paducah Scrap Book over to a Manager, and he Booked them. Zoroaster assured the Manager that Him and his Partner done a Refined Act, suitable for Women and Children, with a strong Finish, which had been the Talk of all Galveston. The Manager put them in between the Trained Ponies and a Legit with a Bad Cold. When a Legit loses his Voice he goes into Vodeville.

Zoroaster and Zendavesta came on very Cocky, and for the 7,800th Time Zoroaster asked Zendavesta:

"Who wuz it I seen you comin' up the Street with?"

Then, for the 7,800th Time, by way of Mirth-Provoking Re-joinder, Zendavesta kicked Zoroaster in the Stomach, after which the Slap-Stick was introduced as a Sub-Motive.

The Manager gave a Sign and the Stage Hands Closed in on the Best Team in the Business, Bar None.

Of course Zoroaster and Zendavesta were very sore at having their Act killed. They said it was no way to treat Artists. The Manager told them they were too Tart for words to tell it and to

ZENDAVESTA

consider Themselves set back into the Supper Show. Then They saw through the whole Conspiracy. The Manager was Mansfield's Friend and Mansfield was out with his Hammer.

At Present they are doing Two Supper Turns to the Piano Player and a Day Watchman. They are still the Best in the Business, but are being used Dead Wrong. However, they derive some Comfort from reading the Paducah Notice.

MORAL: *A Dramatic Editor should never go to a Burgoo Picnic —especially in Kentucky.*

THE FABLE *OF* FLORA *AND* ADOLPH *AND A* HOME GONE WRONG

ONE morning a Modern Solomon, who had been chosen to preside as Judge in a Divorce Mill, climbed to his Perch and unbuttoned his Vest for the Wearisome Grind. He noticed that the first Case looming up on the Docket was that of Flora Botts vs. Adolph Botts.

The Applicant, Mrs. Botts, and Adolph, the Other Half of the Domestic Sketch, were already inside the Railing, each attempting to look the other out of Countenance.—

"Break!" ordered the Judge, "Don't act as if you were at Home. Now, what has Adolph been doing?"

It seemed that she alleged Cruelty, Neglect, Inhuman Treatment, Violent Temper, Threats, etc., etc.

"We have no Chills-and-Fever Music to lend Effect to the Sad Narrative you are about to Spring," said the Judge, looking down at the Plaintiff, who belonged to the Peroxide Tribe. "Furthermore, we will take it for granted that when you first met Defendant your Innocence and Youth made it a Walkaway for his Soft Approaches, and that you had every Reason to believe that he was a Perfect Gentleman. Having disposed of these Preliminaries, let us have the Plot of the Piece."

So she told her Story in a Tremulous, Viola Allen kind of Voice, while her Lawyer wept.

He was ready to Weep for anyone who would hand him $8. Afterthought—make it $7.50.

It was a Dark Tale of how Botts, the Viperish Defendant, had Sneered at her, called her Oh-Such-Names, humiliated her in the presence of Callers, and nagged her with Sarcastic Comments until her Tender Sensibilities had been worn to a Frazzle.

Then the Defendant went on the Stand and entered a General Denial. He had been all that a Rattling Good Husband could be, but she had been a regular Rudyard Kipling Vampire. She had continued to make his Life one lingering Day-After of Regret.

43

His Record for Patience and Long-Suffering had made Job's Performance look like an Amateur's Half-Try.

"There is more in this Case than appears on the Surface," said the Modern Solomon. "In order to fix the Blame we shall have to dig up the First Cause. I will ask Chemical Flora to tell us the Story of her Past Life."

MODERN SOLOMON

"My Parents were Poor, but Refined," said Mrs. Botts. "They gave me Every Advantage. After I finished the High School I attended a Conservatory, and every one said I had Talent. I should have been an Elocutionist. Once I went to Rockford and recited 'The Tramp's Story' at a Club Social, and I got a Lovely Notice. I am especially good at Dialect Recitations."

"Humorous?" asked the Court.

THE VIPER

"Yes, sir; but I can turn right around and be Pathetic all of a sudden, if I want to be."

"I suppose that Botts, after he had lived with you for awhile, didn't have any Hankering Desire to hear you Recite," suggested the Modern Solomon.

"That's just it. When I'd offer to get up in Company and speak Something he'd ask me please not to Recite, and if I had to make a Show of myself, for God's Sake not to tackle anything Humorous, with a Conservatory Dialect to it."

"But you wouldn't let him Stop you?"

"Not on your Life."

"I'd believe you, even if you wasn't under Oath. Now, will Mr. Botts answer me one Question? Has he any Ambition on the Side?"

"Although I am a Bookkeeper for a Gravel-Roofing Concern, I have always believed I could Write," replied Adolph Botts. "About four years ago I began to prepare the Book for a Comic Opera. A Friend of mine who works in a Hat Store was to Compose the Music. I think he has more Ability than Victor Herbert."

"Did this Friend think Well of your Libretto?" asked the Wise Judge.

"Yes, sir; he said it was the Best Thing that had been done since 'Erminie.' In fact, everybody liked my Book."

"Except your Wife," suggested the Court.

"That's it, exactly. I wanted Sympathy and Encouragement and she gave me the Metallic Laugh. There is one Patter Song in my Opera that Every One who comes to my House has been Crazy to hear. Whenever I started to Sing it she would talk in a loud Voice. She never seemed to Appreciate my Stuff. I think the Bleach affected her Head."

"Has the Opera been produced?" asked the Court, with Humane Hesitancy.

"No, the Eastern Managers were all tied up with Harry B. Smith," replied Mr. Botts. "Then there's a Prejudice against Western Talent."

"Well, Mr. Botts, in View of all the Evidence, I have decided to give you a Decree of Divorce from Flo of the Wheaten Tresses," said the Modern Solomon.

"But look here!" exclaimed the Defendant, "I haven't applied for any Divorce."

"You don't have to. I give it to you anyway. As for you, Mrs. Botts, I will give you a Decree also. The Alimony will be $25 per."

"Thanks."

CHEMICAL FLORA

"I don't think you grasp the Decision. When I say that the Alimony is $25 per, I mean that Mrs. Botts will be required to pay that Amount to Adolph every week."

"Shameful!"

"Don't be too hasty. I further Decree that Mr. Botts must pay the same Amount to Flora every Week."

"That simply makes it a Stand-Off," remarked Mr. Botts, who was puzzled.

"My idea of the Case, neatly expressed," said the Modern Solomon. "Each of you is Divorced from the Other, and if Either of you ever Marries again, He or She will be jerked before this Tribunal and sentenced to Ten Years of Hard Labor in some Penal Institution."

Whereupon the Court took a Noon Recess of $3\frac{1}{2}$ hours.

MORAL: *Genius must ever walk Alone.*

THE FABLE OF THE COPPER AND THE JOVIAL UNDERGRADS

ONE Night three Well-Bred Young Men, who were entertained at the Best Houses wherever they went, started out to Wreck a College town.

The licked two Hackmen, set fire to an Awning, pulled down many Signs, and sent a Brick through the Front Window of a Tailor Shop. All the Residents of the Town went into their Houses and locked the Doors; Terror brooded over the Community.

A Copper heard the Racket, and saw Women and Children fleeing to Places of Safety, so he gripped his Club and ran Ponderously, overtaking the three Well-Bred Young Men in a dark part of the Street, where they were Engaged in tearing down a Fence.

He could not see them Distinctly, and he made the Mistake of assuming that they were Drunken Ruffians from the Iron Foundry. So he spoke harshly, and told them to Leave Off breaking the Man's Fence. His Tone and Manner irritated the University Men, who were not accustomed to Rudeness from Menials.

One Student, who wore a Sweater, and whose people butt into the Society Column with Sickening Regularity, started to Tackle Low; he had Bushy Hair and a Thick Neck, and his strong Specialty was to swing on Policemen and Cabbies.

At this, his Companion, whose Great Grandmother had been one of the eight thousand Close Relatives of John Randolph, asked him not to Kill the Policeman. He said the Fellow had made a Mistake, that was all; they were not Muckers; they were Nice Boys, intent on preserving the Traditions of dear old *Alma Mater*.

The Copper could hardly Believe it until they led him to a Street Lamp, and showed him their Engraved Cards and Junior Society Badges; then he Realized that they were All Right. The third Well-Bred Young Man, whose Male Parent got his Coin

by wrecking a Building Association in Chicago, then announced
that they were Gentlemen, and could Pay for everything they
broke. Thus it will be seen that they were Rollicking College Boys
and not Common Rowdies.

The Copper, perceiving that he had come very near getting Gay
with our First Families, Apologized for Cutting In. The Well-
Bred Young Men forgave him, and then took his Club away
from him, just to Demonstrate that there were no Hard Feelings.
On the way back to the Seat of Learning they captured a Night
Watchman, and put him down a Man-Hole.

MORAL: *Always select the Right Sort of Parents before you
start in to be Rough.*

STUDENT

THE FABLE *OF THE* PROFESSOR *WHO* WANTED *TO BE* ALONE

NOW it happens that in America a man who goes up hanging to a Balloon is a Professor.

One day a Professor, preparing to make a Grand Ascension, was sorely pestered by Spectators of the Yellow-Hammer Variety, who fell over the Stay-Ropes or crowded up close to the Balloon to ask Fool Questions. They wanted to know how fur up he Calkilated to go and was he Afeerd and how often had he did it. The Professor answered them in the Surly Manner peculiar to Showmen accustomed to meet a Web-Foot Population. On the Q. T. the Prof. had Troubles of his own. He was expected to drop in at a Bank on the following Day and take up a Note for 100 Plunks. The Ascension meant 50 to him, but how to Corral the other 50? That was the Hard One.

This question was in his Mind as he took hold of the Trapeze Bar and signaled the Farm Hands to let go. As he trailed Skyward beneath the buoyant silken Bag he hung by his Knees and waved a glad Adieu to the Mob of Inquisitive Yeomen. A Sense of Relief came to him as he saw the Crowd sink away in the Distance.

Hanging by one Toe, and with his right Palm presssed to his Eyes, he said: "Now that I am Alone, let me Think, let me Think."

There in the Vast Silence He Thought.

Presently he gave a sigh of Relief.

"I will go to my Wife's Brother and make a Quick Touch," he said. "If he refuses to Unbelt I will threaten to tell his Wife of the bracelet he bought in Louisville."

Having reached this Happy Conclusion, he loosened the Parachute and quickly descended to the Earth.

MORAL: *Avoid Crowds.*

THE PROFESSOR

THE FABLE *OF A* STATESMAN *WHO* COULDN'T MAKE GOOD

ONCE there was a Bluff whose Long Suit was Glittering Generalities.

He hated to Work and it hurt his Eyes to read Law, but on a Clear Day he could be heard a Mile, so he became a Statesman.

Whenever the Foresters had a Picnic they invited him to make the Principal Address, because he was the only Orator who could beat out the Merry-Go-Round.

The Habit of Dignity enveloped him.

Upon his Brow Deliberation sat. He wore a Fireman's moustache and a White Lawn Tie, and he loved to Talk about the Flag.

At a Clam-Bake in 1884 he hurled Defiance at all the Princes and Potentates of Europe, and the Sovereign Voters, caught up by his Matchless Eloquence and Unswerving Courage, elected him to the Legislature.

While he was in the Legislature he discovered that these United States were an Asylum for the Down-Trodden and oppressed of the Whole World, and frequently called Attention to the Fact. When some one asked him if he was cutting up any Easy Money or would it be safe for a Man with a Watch to go to Sleep in the same Room with him, he would take a Drink of Water and begin to plead for Cuba.

Once an Investigating Committee got after him and he was about to be Shown Up for Dallying with Corporations, but he put on a fresh White Tie and made a Speech about our Heroic Dead on a Hundred Battle-Fields, and Most People said it was simply Impossible for such a Thunderous Patriot to be a Crook. So he played the Glittering Generality stronger than ever.

In Due Time he Married a Widow of the Bantam Division. The Reason she married him was that he looked to her to be a Coming Congressman and she wanted to get a Whack at Washington Society. Besides, she lived in a Flat and the Janitor would not permit her to keep a Dog.

About Ten Days after they were Married he came Home at

4 A. M. in a Sea-Going Hack and he was Saturated. Next Morning she had him up on the Carpet and wanted to know How About It.

He arose and put his Right Hand inside of his Prince Albert Coat and began.

"Madam," he said, "During a Long, and, I trust, a not altogether fruitless Career as a Servant of the Peepul, I have always

STATESMAN

stood in the Fierce Light of Publicity, and my Record is an Open Book which he who runs may——"

"Nix! Nix!" she said, rapping for order with a Tea-Cup. "Let go of the Flying Rings. Get back to the Green Earth!"

He dilated his Nostrils and said: "From the Rock-Bound Hills of Maine in the North to the Everglades of Florida——"

"Forget the Everglades," she said, rapping again. "That Super-heated Atmosphere may have a certain Tonic Effect on the Hydro-cephalous Voter, but if you want to adjust yourself with Wifey, you come down to Cases."

So he went out after Breakfast and bought a $22 Hat in order to Square himself.

MORAL: *Some Women should be given the Right to Vote.*

THE BANTAM

THE FABLE *OF THE* BRASH DRUMMER *AND* THE PEACH *WHO* LEARNED *THAT* THERE WERE OTHERS

A WELL-FIXED Mortgage Shark, residing at a Way Station, had a Daughter whose Experience was not as large as her prospective Bank Roll. She had all the component Parts of a Peach, but she didn't know how to make a Showing, and there was nobody in Town qualified to give her a quiet Hunch.

She got her Fashion Hints from a Trade Catalogue, and took her Tips on Etiquette and Behavior from the Questions and Answers Department of an Agricultural Monthly.

The Girl and her Father lived in a big White House, with Evergreen Trees and whitewashed Dornicks in front of it, and a Wind-Pump at the rear. Father was a good deal the same kind of a Man as David Harum, except that he didn't let go of any Christmas Presents, or work the Soft Pedal when he had a chance to apply a Crimp to some Widow who had seen Better Days. In fact, Daughter was the only one on Earth who could induce him to Loosen Up.

Now, it happened that there came to this Town every Thirty Days a brash Drummer, who represented a Tobacco House. He was a Gabby Young Man, and he could Articulate at all Times, whether he had anything to Say or not.

One night, at a Lawn Fête given by the Ladies of the Methodist Congregation, he met Daughter. She noticed that his Trousers did not bag at the Knees; also that he wore a superb Ring. They strolled under the Maples, and he talked what is technically known as Hot Air. He made an Impression considerably deeper than himself. She promised to Correspond.

On the occasion of his next Visit to the Way Station, he let her wear his Ring, and made a Wish, while she took him riding in the Phaeton. He began to carry her Photograph in his Watch, and show it to the Boys employed at the House. Sometimes he would fold over one of her Letters so they could see how it started out. He said the Old Man had Nothing But, and he pro-

posed to make it a case of Marry. Truly, it seemed that he was the
principal Cake in the Pantry, and little did he suspect that he
could be Frosted.

But Daughter, after much Pleading, induced Father to send
her to a Finishing School in the East. (A Finishing School is a
Place at which Young Ladies are taught how to give the Quick
Finish to all Persons who won't do.)

DAUGHTER

At School, the Daughter tied up with a Chum, who seldom over-looked a Wednesday Matinee, and she learned more in three Weeks than her Childhood Home could have shown her in three Centuries.

Now she began to see the other Kind; the Kind that Wears a Cutaway, with a White Flower, in the Morning, a Frock, with Violets, in the Afternoon, and a jimmy little Tuxedo at Night.

For the first time she began to listen to Harness that had Chains to it, and she rode in Vehicles that permitted her to glance in at the Second Stories.

She stopped wearing Hats, and began to choose Confections. She selected them Languidly, three at a time.

Then the Bill to the Way Station, and Father down with Heart Failure.

She kept Mr. Sothern's Picture on her Dresser, with two Red Candles burning in front of it, and every time she thought of Gabby Will, the Crackerjack Salesman, she reached for the Peau d'Espagne and sprayed herself.

*   *   *

One Day when the Tobacco Salesman came up Main Street with his Grips, on his way to visit the Trade, he met the Drug Clerk, who told him that She was Home on a Visit. So he hurried through with his Work, got a Shave, changed ends on his Cuffs, pared his Nails, bought a box of Marshmallows, and went out to the House.

Daughter was on the Lawn, seated under a Canopy that had set Father back thirty-two Dollars. There was a Hired Hand sprinkling the Grass with a Hose, and as Will, the Conversa-tional Drummer, came up the Long Walk, Daughter called to the Hired Hand, and said: "Johnson, there is a Strange Man coming up the Walk; change the Direction of the Stream some-what, else you may Dampen him."

The Drummer approached her, feeling of his Necktie, and wondered if she would up and Kiss him, right in broad Daylight. She didn't. Daughter allowed a rose-colored Booklet, by Guy de Maupassant, to sink among the Folds of her French Gown, and then she Looked at him, and said: "All Goods must be delivered at the Rear."

"Don't you Know me?" he asked.

"Rully, it seems to me I have seen you, Somewhere," she replied, "but I cahn't place you. Are you the Man who tunes the Piano?"

"Don't you remember the night I met you at the Lawn Fete?" he asked; and then, Chump that he was, and all Rattled, he told her his Name, instead of giving her the scorching Come-Back that he composed next Day, when it was Too Late.

IN THE EAST

"I meet so many People traveling about," she said; "I cahn't remember all of them, you know. I dare say you called to see Pu-pah; he will be here Presently."

Then she gave him "Some one's else," "Neyether," "Savoir-Faire," and a few other Crisp Ones, hot from the Finishing School, after which she asked him how the Dear Villagers were coming on. He reminded her that he did not live in the Town. She said: "Only Fahncy!" and he said he guessed he'd have to be Going, as he had promised a Man to meet him at Jordan's Store before the Bank closed.

As he moved toward the St. Nicholas Hotel he kept his Hand on his Solar Plexus. At five o'clock he rode out of Town on a Local.

MORAL: *Anybody can Win unless there happens to be a Second Entry.*

A STRANGE MAN

THE FABLE *OF* SISTER MAE, *WHO* DID *AS* WELL *AS* COULD BE EXPECTED

TWO Sisters lived in Chicago, the Home of Opportunity.
Luella was a Good Girl, who had taken Prizes at the Mission Sunday School, but she was Plain, much. Her Features did not seem to know the value of Team Work. Her Clothes fit her Intermittently, as it were. She was what would be called a Lumpy Dresser. But she had a good Heart.

Luella found Employment at a Hat Factory. All she had to do was to put Red Linings in Hats for the Country Trade; and every Saturday Evening when Work was called on account of Darkness, the Boss met her as she went out and crowded three Dollars on her.

The other Sister was Different.

She began as Mary, then changed to Marie, and her Finish was Mae.

From earliest Youth she had lacked Industry and Application. She was short on Intellect but long on Shape.

The Vain Pleasures of the World attracted her. By skipping the Long Words she could read how Rupert Bansiford led Sibyl Gray into the Conservatory and made Love that scorched the Begonias. Sometimes she just Ached to light out with an Opera Company.

When she couldn't stand up Luella for any more Car Fare she went out looking for Work, and hoping she wouldn't find it. The sagacious Proprietor of a Lunch Room employed her as Cashier. In a little While she learned to count Money, and could hold down the Job.

Marie was a Strong Card. The Male Patrons of the Establishment hovered around the Desk long after paying their Checks. Within a Month the Receipts of the Place had doubled.

It was often remarked that Marie was a Pippin. Her Date Book had to be kept on the Double Entry System.

Although her Grammar was Sad, it made no Odds. Her Picture was on many a Button.

A Credit Man from the Wholesale House across the Street told her that any time she wanted to see the Telegraph Poles rush past, she could tear Transportation out of his Book. But Marie turned him down for a Bucket Shop Man, who was not Handsome, but was awful Generous.

They were Married, and went to live in a Flat with a Quarter-Sawed Oak Chiffonier and Pink Rugs. She was Mae at this Stage of the Game.

THE BOSS

Shortly after this, Wheat jumped twenty-two points, and the Husband didn't do a thing.

Mae bought a Thumb Ring and a Pug Dog, and began to speak of the Swede Help as "The Maid."

Then she decided that she wanted to live in a House, because, in a Flat, One could never be sure of One's Neighbors. So they moved into a Sarcophagus on the Boulevard, right in between two Old Families, who had made their Money soon after the Fire, and Ice began to form on the hottest Days.

Mae bought an Automobile, and blew her Allowance against Beauty Doctors. The Smell of Cooking made her Faint, and she couldn't see where the Working Classes came in at all.

When she attended the theater a Box was none too good. Husband went along, in evening clothes and a Yachting Cap, and he had two large Diamonds in his Shirt Front.

Sometimes she went to a Vogner Concert, and sat through it, and she wouldn't Admit any more that the Russell Brothers, as the Irish Chambermaids, hit her just about Right.

She was determined to break into Society if she had to use an Ax.

At last she Got There; but it cost her many a Reed Bird and several Gross of Cold Quarts.

In the Hey-Day of Prosperity did Mae forget Luella? No, indeed.

She took Luella away from the Hat Factory, where the Pay was three Dollars a Week, and gave her a Position as Assistant Cook at five Dollars.

MORAL: *Industry and Perseverance bring a sure Reward.*

MAE

THE FABLE *OF* HOW *THE* FOOL-KILLER
BACKED OUT *OF A* CONTRACT

THE Fool-Killer came along the Pike Road one Day and stopped to look at a Strange Sight.

Inside of a Barricade were several Thousands of Men, Women and Children. They were moving restlessly among the trampled Weeds, which were clotted with Watermelon Rinds, Chicken Bones, Straw and torn Paper Bags.

It was a very hot Day. The People could not sit down. They shuffled Wearily and were pop-eyed with Lassitude and Discouragement.

A stifling Dust enveloped them. They Gasped and Sniffled. Some tried to alleviate their Sufferings by gulping down a Pink Beverage made of Drug-Store Acid, which fed the Fires of Thirst.

Thus they wove and interwove in the smoky Oven. The Whimper or the faltering Wail of Children, the quavering Sigh of overlaced Women, and the long-drawn Profanity of Men—these were what the Fool-Killer heard as he looked upon the Suffering Throng.

"Is this a new Wrinkle on Dante's Inferno?" he asked of the Man on the Gate, who wore a green Badge marked "Marshal," and was taking Tickets.

"No, sir; this is a County Fair," was the reply.

"Why do the People congregate in the Weeds and allow the Sun to warp them?"

"Because Everybody does it."

"Do they Pay to get in?"

"You know it."

"Can they Escape?"

"They can, but they prefer to Stick."

The Fool-Killer hefted his Club and then looked at the Crowd and shook his Head doubtfully.

"I can't tackle that Outfit to-day," he said. "It's too big a Job."

So he went on into Town, and singled out a Main Street Merchant who refused to Advertise.

MORAL: *People who expect to be Luny will find it safer to travel in a Bunch.*

THE FOOL-KILLER

THE FABLE *OF THE* CADDY *WHO* HURT HIS HEAD WHILE THINKING

ONE Day a Caddy sat in the Long Grass near the Ninth Hole and wondered if he had a Soul. His Number was 27, and he almost had forgotten his Real Name.

As he sat and Meditated, two Players passed him. They were going the Long Round, and the Frenzy was upon them.

They followed the Gutta Percha Balls with the intent swiftness of trained Bird Dogs, and each talked feverishly of Brassy Lies, and getting past the Bunker, and Lofting to the Green, and Slicing into the Bramble—each telling his own Game to the Ambient Air, and ignoring what the other Fellow had to say.

As they did the St. Andrews Full Swing for eighty Yards apiece and then Followed Through with the usual Explanations of how it Happened, the Caddy looked at them and Reflected that they were much inferior to his Father.

His Father was too Serious a Man to get out in Mardi Gras Clothes and hammer a Ball from one Red Flag to another.

His Father worked in a Lumber Yard.

He was an Earnest Citizen, who seldom Smiled, and he knew all about the Silver Question and how J. Pierpont Morgan done up a Free People on the Bond Issue.

The Caddy wondered why it was that his Father, a really Great Man, had to shove Lumber all day and could seldom get one Dollar to rub against another, while these superficial Johnnies who played Golf all the Time had Money to Throw at the Birds. The more he Thought the more his Head ached.

MORAL: *Don't try to Account for Anything.*

MEDITATIVE CADDY

THE FABLE *OF THE* MARTYR *WHO* LIKED *THE* JOB

O NCE in a Country Town there was a Man with a Weak Back.

He could put a Grindstone into a Farm Wagon if any one wanted to bet him the Segars, but every time he lifted an Ax, something caught him right in the Spine and he had to go into the House and lie down. So his Wife took Boarders and did the Cooking herself.

He was willing to divide the Labor, however; so he did the Marketing. Only, when he had bought the Victuals, he would squat on a Shoe-Box with the Basket between his Legs and say that he couldn't see what Congress wuz thinkin' of.

He had certain Theories in regard to the Alaskan Boundary and he was against any Anglo-American Alliance becuz Uncle Sam could take care of himself at any Turn in the Road, comin' right down to it, and the American People wuz superior to any other Naytionality in every Way, Shape, Manner and Form, as fur as that's concerned. Then his Wife would have to send Word for him to come on with the Groceries so she could get Dinner.

Nearly Everybody Sympathized with her, because she had to put up with such a big Hulk of a no-account Husband. She was looked upon as a Martyr.

One Day the Husband was Sunstruck, being too Lazy to move into the Shade, and next Day he Passed Away without an Effort. The Widow gave him the best Funeral of the Year and then put all the Money she could rake and scrape into a Marble Shaft marked "At Rest."

A good many People said she was Better Off without him, and it was certainly a Good Riddance of Bad Rubbish.

They hoped that if she ever Married again she'd pick out Somebody that wuzn't afraid to Work, and had Gumption enough to pound Sand into a Rat-Hole.

There was General Satisfaction when she became the Wife of Mr. Gladden, who owned the General Store. He built a new House, hired a Girl and had the Washing sent out. She could go into the Store and pick out Anything she wanted, and he took her riding in his new Runabout every Evening.

Consequently, she was very Miserable, thinking of the Jewel she had lost.

MORAL: *If the Woman thinks he's All Right, you keep on your own Side of the Fence.*

A MARTYR

THE FABLE OF THE BOHEMIAN WHO HAD HARD LUCK

ONCE upon a Time there was a Brilliant but Unappreciated Chap who was such a Thorough Bohemian that Strangers usually mistook him for a Tramp.

Would he brush his Clothes? Not he. When he wore a Collar he was Ashamed of himself. He had Pipe-Ashes on his Coat and Vest. He seldom Combed his Hair, and never Shaved.

Every Evening he ate an Imitation Dinner, at a forty-cent Table d'Hôte, with a Bottle of Writing Fluid thrown in. He had formed a little Salon of Geniuses, who also were out of Work, and they loved to Loll around on their Shoulder-Blades and Laugh Bitterly at the World.

The main Bohemian was an Author. After being Turned Down by numerous Publishers, he had decided to write for Posterity. Posterity hadn't heard anything about it, and couldn't get out an Injunction.

He knew his Works were good, because all the Free and Untrammeled Souls in the Spaghetti Joint told him so. He would read them a Little Thing of his Own about Wandering in the Fields with Lesbia, and then he would turn to a Friend, whose Face was all covered with Human Ivy, and ask him, point blank: "Is it, or is it not, Better than the Dooley Stuff?"

"There is no Comparison," would be the Reply, coming through the Foliage.

Wandering in the Fields with Lesbia! Lesbia would have done Well. If he had Wandered in the Fields at any Time he would have been Pinched on Suspicion that he was out for Turnips.

The sure-enough Bohemian was a Scathing Critic. If Brander Matthews only knew some of the Things said about him, there would be Tear Marks on his Pillow. And Howells, too. Bah! My, but he was Caustic.

The way he burned up Magazine Writers, it's a Wonder they didn't get after him for Arson.

One day, while standing on the Front Stoop at his Boarding House, trying to think of some one who would submit to a Touch, a Flower Pot fell from a Window Ledge above him, and hit him on the Head. He was put into an Ambulance and taken to a Hospital, where the Surgeons clipped his Hair short, in order to take Three Stitches. While he was still Unconscious, and therefore unable to Resist, they Scrubbed him with Castile Soap, gave him a good Shave, and put him into a snowy-white Gown.

His Friends heard of the Accident, and went to the Hospital to offer Condolence. When they found him he was so Clean and Commonplace that they lost all Respect for him.

MORAL: *Get a good Make-Up and the Part plays itself.*

THOROUGH BOHEMIAN

THE FABLE *OF THE* COMING CHAMPION *WHO WAS* DELAYED

IN a certain Athletic Club which rented two rooms over a Tin-Shop there was one Boy who could put it All Over the other Members.

He knew how to Jab and Counter and Upper-Cut and Bore in with the Left and Play for the Wind. He had Lumps on his Arms and a good Pair of Shoulders, and every one in the Club told him he had the makings of a World-Beater. He used to coax Grocery Clerks and Grammar-School Children to put on the Gloves with him, and then he would go around them, like a Cooper around a Barrel, and Trim them right and proper.

His friends would stand and watch him make Monkeys of these anæmic Amateurs, and gradually the Conviction grew within them that he could Lick anybody of his Weight. The Boy believed them when they told him he ought to go after the Top-Notchers.

He gave up his Job in the Planing Mill and became a Pugilist. The Proprietor of a Cigar Store acted as his Manager, and began to pay his Board. This Manager was Foxy. He told the Boy that before tackling the Championship Class it would be better to go out and beat a lot of Fourth-Raters, thereby building up a Reputation and at the same time getting here and there a Mess of the Long Green.

In the same Town there was an Undertaker who had Sporting Blood in his Veins, and he sought out the Manager and made a Match in behalf of an Unknown.

The boy went into Training in a Stable. He had a yellow Punching Bag, a Sponge, a Bath-Robe and several Towels. Two Paper-Hangers who were out of Work acted as his Trainers. They rubbed him with Witch Hazel all day, and in the Evening the Boy stood around in a Sweater and Talked out of the corner of his Mouth. He said he was Trained to the Minute, as Hard as Nails and Fit as a Fiddle, and he would make Mr. Unknown jump out of the Ring.

As the Day of the Battle approached it came out that the Unknown was a Scrapper who had been fairly Successful at one Time, but had ceased to be a Live One several Years before. He was imported especially for this Contest with the Coming Champion.

When he arrived in Town it was evident that he lacked Condition. He had been dieting himself on Pie and Beer, and any Expert, such as the Cigar Store Man, could tell by looking at

MANAGER

him that his Abdomen was not hard enough to withstand those crushing Body Blows such as the Boy was in the Habit of Landing —on the Punching Bag. Accordingly the Word went around that the imported Pug was too Fat and had bad Wind.

It began to resemble a Cinch.

The Manager went out and bet more Money, and the Coming Champion was Nervous for fear that he would kill the Has-Been if he connected too strong on the Point of the Jaw. He thought it would be better to wear him down with Short-Arm blows and make him Quit. He had read that it was Dangerous to punish a Physical Wreck, who might have Heart Trouble or something like that. The Boy was a Professional Pugilist, but he had Humane Instincts.

When the Boy came to the Train which was to carry the Participants and the Spectators to the Battle-Field he was attended by four Comrades, who had Ice, Beef Tea, Brandy, Alcohol, Blankets and other Paraphernalia. They made a Couch for him in the Baggage Car, and had him lie down, so that he might conserve all his Strength and step into the Ring as fresh as possible. The so-called Unknown had no one to Handle him. He sat Alone in the Men's Car, with a queer Telescope Valise on his Knees, and he smoked a Cigarette, which was in direct Violation of all the Rules of Training.

At last the Company arrived at the Secluded Spot, and a Ring was staked out.

The Coming Champion was received with Loud Cheers. He wore a new Pair of Gymnasium Shoes, spotless Trunks, and around his Waist was an American Flag, presented by his Admirers in the Athletic Club.

In a few Moments the Imported Scrapper came into the Ring, attended by the Sporty Undertaker. He wore an old Pair of Bike Shoes and faded Work Trousers, chopped off at the Knees, while his Belt was a Shawl-Strap. He was chewing Gum.

After he put on the Gloves he looked over at the Coming Champion and remarked to the Undertaker that he (the Coming Champion) seemed to be a Nice Young Fellow. After which he Yawned slightly, and wanted to know what Time they would get a Train back to Town.

The Bell rang, and there in the Center of the Ring stood the Tottering Has-Been and the Coming Champion.

The Has-Been was crouched, with his Head drawn in, turtle-fashion, his Legs spraddled, and oh, the hard, vicious Expression on that Face, as he Fiddled Short and looked intently at the Coming Champion's Feet. This was a very confusing and un-

THE COMING CHAMPION

professional Thing to do, as the Boy had not been accustomed to boxing with People who looked at his Feet. He wondered if there was anything the matter with his Gymnasium Shoes.

In a Moment or two he saw that the Physical Wreck was afraid to Lead, so he did some nimble Foot Work, and his Gloves began to describe Parabolas—then all at once somebody turned off the Sunshine.

They threw Cold Water on him, held a Bottle of Ammonia to his Nose and stuck Pins in under his Finger-Nails.

At last his Eye-Lids fluttered, and he turned a dim and filmy Gaze on his faithful Seconds gathered about him.

"Oh, how the Birds sing!" he murmured. "And see! The Aurora Borealis is trying to climb over Pain's Fire-Works."

"Cheer up!" said the Manager. "He took a Mean Advantage of you and Hit you when you wasn't Looking."

"Ah yes, it all comes back to me. Did I win?"

"Not quite," replied the Manager, who feared to tell him the whole Truth.

"You say he Hit me?" asked the Coming Champion.

"Yes."

"With a Casting?"

"We couldn't tell. He was in such a Hurry."

All this Time the Victor was sitting on the Station Platform with the Undertaker. He was Remarking that it seemed to be a very Purty Country thereabouts, and he'd often wished he could close in on enough of the Gilt to buy him a nice piece of Land somewhere, inasmuch as he regarded a Farmer as the most independent Man on Earth.

Next week there was a familiar Name back on the Time-Card at the Planing Mill.

MORAL: *In all the Learned Professions, Many are Called but Few are Chosen.*

AND SEE!

THE FABLE OF THE LAWYER WHO BROUGHT IN A MINORITY REPORT

AT a Bazaar, the purpose of which was to Hold Up the Public for the Benefit of a Worthy Cause, there were many Schemes to induce Visitors to let go of their Assets. One of the most likely Grafts perpetrated by the astute Management was a Voting Contest to Determine who was the Most Beautiful and Popular Young Lady in the City. It cost Ten Cents to cast one Vote. The Winner of the Contest was to receive a beautiful Vase, with Roses on it.

A prominent Young Lawyer, who was Eloquent, Good Looking, and a Leader in Society, had been selected to make the Presentation Speech after the Votes had been counted.

In a little while the Contest had narrowed down until it was Evident that either the Brewer's Daughter or the Contractor's Daughter was the Most Beautiful and Popular Young Lady in the City. The Brewer and his Friends pushed Ten Dollar Bills into the Ballot Box, while the Contractor, just before the Polls closed, slipped in a Check for One Hundred Dollars.

When the Votes were counted, the Management of the Bazaar was pleased to learn that the Sixty-Cent Vase had Netted over Seven Hundred Dollars. It was Announced that the Contractor's Daughter was exactly Nine Dollars and Twenty Cents more Beautiful and Popular than the Brewer's Daughter.

Thereupon the Committee requested that the Eloquent Young Lawyer step to the Rostrum and make the Presentation Speech. There was no Response; the Young Lawyer had Disappeared.

One of the Members of the Committee started on a Search for him, and found him in a dusky Corner of the Japanese Tea Garden, under the Paper Lanterns, making a Proposal of Marriage to a Poor Girl who had not received one Vote.

MORAL: *Never believe a Relative.*

THE MINORITY REPORT

THE FABLE *OF THE TWO* MANDOLIN PLAYERS *AND* THE WILLING PERFORMER

A VERY attractive Debutante knew two Young Men who called on her every Thursday Evening, and brought their Mandolins along.

They were Conventional Young Men, of the Kind that you see wearing Spring Overcoats in the Clothing Advertisements. One was named Fred, and the other was Eustace.

The Mothers of the Neighbourhood often remarked, "What Perfect Manners Fred and Eustace have!" Merely as an aside it may be added that Fred and Eustace were more Popular with the Mothers than they were with the Younger Set, although no one could say a Word against either of them. Only it was rumored in Keen Society that they didn't Belong. The Fact that they went Calling in a Crowd, and took their Mandolins along, may give the Acute Reader some Idea of the Life that Fred and Eustace held out to the Young Women of their Acquaintance.

The Debutante's name was Myrtle. Her Parents were very Watchful, and did not encourage her to receive Callers, except such as were known to be Exemplary Young Men. Fred and Eustace were a few of those who escaped the Black List. Myrtle always appeared to be glad to see them, and they regarded her as a Darned Swell Girl.

Fred's Cousin came from St. Paul on a Visit; and one Day, in the Street, he saw Myrtle, and noticed that Fred tipped his Hat, and gave her a Stage Smile.

"Oh, Queen of Sheba!" exclaimed the Cousin from St. Paul, whose name was Gus, as he stood stock still, and watched Myrtle's Reversible Plaid disappear around a Corner. "She's a Bird. Do you know her well?"

"I know her Quite Well," replied Fred, coldly. "She is a Charming Girl."

"She is all of that. You're a great Describer. And now what Night are you going to take me around to Call on her?"

Fred very naturally Hemmed and Hawed. It must be remembered that Myrtle was a member of an Excellent Family, and had been schooled in the Proprieties, and it was not to be supposed that she would crave the Society of slangy old Gus, who had an abounding Nerve, and furthermore was as Fresh as the Mountain Air.

He was the Kind of Fellow who would see a Girl twice, and then, upon meeting her the Third Time, he would go up and straighten her Cravat for her, and call her by her First Name.

MYRTLE

Put him into a Strange Company—en route to a Picnic—and by the time the Baskets were unpacked he would have a Blonde all to himself, and she would have traded her Fan for his College Pin.

If a Fair-Looker on the Street happened to glance at him Hard he would run up and seize her by the Hand, and convince her that they had Met. And he always Got Away with it, too.

In a Department Store, while waiting for the Cash Boy to come back with the Change, he would find out the Girl's Name, her Favourite Flower, and where a Letter would reach her.

Upon entering a Parlor Car at St. Paul he would select a Chair next to the Most Promising One in Sight, and ask her if she cared to have the Shade lowered.

Before the Train cleared the Yards he would have the Porter bringing a Foot-Stool for the Lady.

At Hastings he would be asking her if she wanted Something to Read.

At Red Wing he would be telling her that she resembled Maxine Elliott, and showing her his Watch, left to him by his Grandfather, a Prominent Virginian.

At La Crosse he would be reading the Menu Card to her, and telling her how different it is when you have Some One to join you in a Bite.

At Milwaukee he would go out and buy a Bouquet for her, and when they rode into Chicago they would be looking out of the same Window, and he would be arranging for her Baggage with the Transfer Man. After that they would be Old Friends.

Now, Fred and Eustace had been at School with Gus, and they had seen his Work, and they were not disposed to Introduce him into One of the most Exclusive Homes in the City.

They had known Myrtle for many Years; but they did not dare to Address her by her First Name, and they were Positive that if Gus attempted any of his usual Tactics with her she would be Offended; and, naturally enough, they would be Blamed for bringing him to the House.

But Gus insisted. He said he had seen Myrtle, and she Suited him from the Ground up, and he proposed to have Friendly Doings with her. At last they told him they would take him if he promised to Behave. Fred warned him that Myrtle would frown down any Attempt to be Familiar on Short Acquaintance, and Eustace said that as long as he had known Myrtle he had never Presumed to be Free and Forward with her. He had simply played the Mandolin. That was as Far Along as he had ever got.

Gus told them not to Worry about him. All he asked was a Start. He said he was a Willing Performer, but as yet he never

FRED AND EUSTACE

had been Disqualified for Crowding. Fred and Eustace took this to mean that he would not Overplay his Attentions, so they escorted him to the House.

As soon as he had been Presented, Gus showed her where to sit on the Sofa, then he placed himself about Six Inches away and began to Buzz, looking her straight in the Eye. He said that when he first saw her he Mistook her for Miss Prentice, who was said to be the Most Beautiful Girl in St. Paul, only, when he came closer, he saw that it couldn't be Miss Prentice, because Miss Prentice didn't have such Lovely Hair. Then he asked her the Month of her Birth and told her Fortune, thereby coming nearer to Holding her Hand within Eight Minutes than Eustace had come in a Lifetime.

"Play something, Boys," he Ordered, just as if he had paid them Money to come along and make Music for him.

They unlimbered their Mandolins and began to play a Sousa March. He asked Myrtle if she had seen the New Moon. She replied that she had not, so they went Outside.

When Fred and Eustace finished the first Piece, Gus appeared at the open Window, and asked them to play "The Georgia Camp-Meeting," which had always been one of his Favorites.

So they played that, and when they had Concluded there came a Voice from the Outer Darkness, and it was the Voice of Myrtle. She said: "I'll tell you what to Play; play the Intermezzo."

Fred and Eustace exchanged Glances. They began to Perceive that they had been backed into a Siding. With a few Potted Palms in front of them, and two Cards from the Union, they would have been just the same as a Hired Orchestra.

But they played the Intermezzo and felt Peevish. Then they went to the Window and looked out. Gus and Myrtle were sitting in the Hammock, which had quite a Pitch toward the Center. Gus had braced himself by Holding to the back of the Hammock. He did not have his Arm around Myrtle, but he had it Extended in a Line parallel with her Back. What he had done wouldn't Justify a Girl in saying, "Sir!" but it started a Real Scandal with Fred and Eustace. They saw that the only Way to Get Even with her was to go Home without saying "Good Night." So they slipped out the Side Door, shivering with Indignation.

After that, for several Weeks, Gus kept Myrtle so Busy that she had no Time to think of considering other Candidates. He sent Books to her Mother, and allowed the Old Gentleman to take Chips away from him at Poker.

They were Married in the Autumn, and Father-in-Law took Gus into the Firm, saying that he had needed a good Pusher for a Long Time.

At the Wedding the two Mandolin Players were permitted to act as Ushers.

MORAL: *To get a fair Trial of Speed, use a Pace-Maker.*

THE WILLING PERFORMER

THE FABLE *OF THE* MAN *WHO* DIDN'T CARE *FOR* STORY-BOOKS

ONCE there was a blue Dyspeptic, who attempted to Kill Time by reading Novels, until he discovered that all Books of Fiction were a Mockery.

After a prolonged Experience he came to know that every Specimen of Light Reading belonged to one of the following Divisions:

1. The Book that Promises well until you reach the Plot, and then you Remember that you read it Summer before last.

2. The book with the Author's Picture as a Frontispiece. The Author is very Cocky. He has his Overcoat thrown back, so as to reveal the Silk Lining. That Settles it!

3. The Book that runs into a Snarl of Dialect on the third Page and never gets out.

4. The delectable Yarn about a Door-Mat Thief, who truly loves the Opium Fiend. Jolly Story of the Slums.

5. The Book that begins with a twenty-page Description of Sloppy Weather: "Long swirls of riven Rain beat somberly upon the misty Panes," etc., etc.

You turn to the last Chapter to see if it Rains all the way through the Book. This last Chapter is a Give-Away. It condenses the whole Plot and dishes up the Conclusion. After that, who would have the Nerve to wade through the Two Hundred and Forty intermediate Pages?

6. The Book in which the Pictures tell the Story. After you have seen the Pictures there is no need to wrestle with the Text.

7. The Book that begins with a Murder Mystery — charming Picture of Gray-Haired Man discovered Dead in his Library — Blood splashed all over the Furniture — Knife of Curious Design lying on Floor.

You know at once that the most Respected and least *sus*pected Personage in the Book committed the awful Crime, but you haven't the Heart to Track him down and compel him to commit Suicide.

8. The Book that gets away with one Man asking another: "By Jove, who is that Dazzling Beauty in the Box?"

The Man who asks this Question has a Name which sounds like the Title of a Sleeping Car.

You feel instinctively that he is going to be all Mixed Up with that Girl in the Box before Chapter XII. is reached; but who can take any real Interest in the Love Affairs of a Man with such a Name?

ALL A MOCKERY

9. The Book that tells all about Society and how Tough it is. Even the Women drink Brandy and Soda, smoke Cigarettes, and Gamble. The clever Man of the World, who says all the Killing Things, is almost as Funny as Ally Sloper. An irritable Person, after reading nine Chapters of this kind of High Life, would be ready to go Home and throw his Grandmother into the Fire.

10. The dull, gray Book, or the Simple Annals of John Gardensass. A Careful Study of American Life.

In Chapter I. he walks along the Lane, stepping first on one Foot and then on the Other, enters a House by the Door, and sits in a four-legged wooden Chair, looking out through a Window with Glass in it. Book denotes careful Observation. Nothing happens until Page 150. Then John decides to sell the Cow. In the Final Chapter he sits on a Fence and Whittles. True Story, but What's the Use?

Why continue? The Dyspeptic said that when he wanted something really Fresh and Original in the Line of Fiction he read the Prospectus of a Mining Corporation.

MORAL: *Only the more Rugged Mortals should attempt to Keep Up on Current Literature.*

MORE
FABLES
IN SLANG

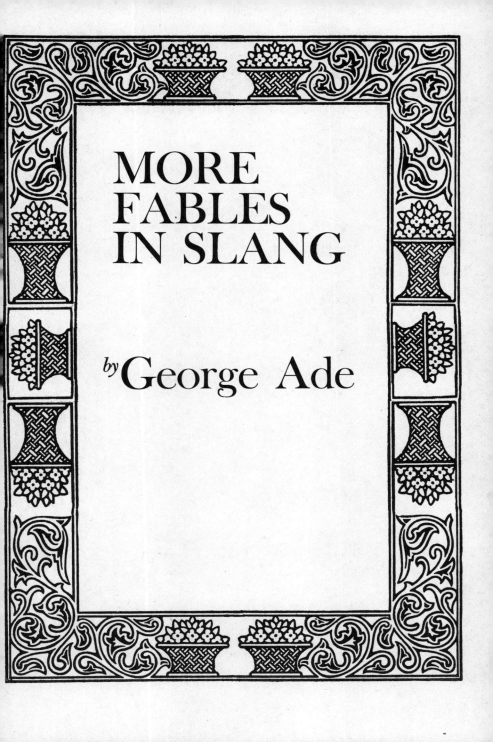

MORE
FABLES
IN SLANG

by George Ade

THE FABLE OF HOW UNCLE BREWSTER WAS TOO SHIFTY FOR THE TEMPTER

WHEN Uncle Brewster had put on his Annual Collar and combed his Beard and was about to start to the Depot, his Wife, Aunt Mehely, looked at him through her Specs and shook her Head doubtfully.

Then she spoke as follows: "You go slow there in the City. You know your Failin's. You're just full of the Old Harry, and when you're Het Up you're just like as not to Raise Ned."

"I guess I can take keer of myse'f about as well as the Next One," retorted Uncle Brewster. "I've been to the Mill an' got my Grist, if any one should ask. I ain't no Greeny."

With that he started for the Train, which was due in one Hour.

As he rode toward the Great City he smoked a Baby Mine Cigar, purchased of the Butcher, and told the Brakeman a few Joe Millers just to throw out the Impression that he was Fine and Fancy.

After he had Registered at the Hotel and Swelled Up properly when addressed as "Mister" by the Clerk, he wanted to know if there was a Lively Show in Town. The Clerk told him to follow the Street until he came to all the Electric Lights, and there he would find a Ballet. Uncle Brewster found the Place, and looked in through the Hole at an Assistant Treasurer, who was Pale and wore a Red Vest.

"I want a Chair near the Band," said Uncle Brewster. "How much does one of 'em Fetch?"

"Two Dollars," replied the Assistant Treasurer, pulling down his Cuffs and then examining himself in a small Mirror at one side of the Diagram.

"Great Grief!" ejaculated Uncle Brewster. "I only paid Thirty-Five Cents for the Glass Blowers, an' I'll warrant you they beat your Troupe as bad as Cranberries beats Glue. I'll see you plumb in Halifax before I—"

"Stand aside, please," said the Assistant Treasurer.

Uncle Brewster saw a Policeman, and thought it his Duty to

tell the Officer that the Theater Folks were a Pack of Robbers.

"Up an Alley," said the Policeman.

Instead of going to a Show, Uncle Brewster stood in front of a Clothing Store and watched the Wax Figures.

When he got back to his Room the Bell-Hopper came around and asked him if he cared to Sit in a Quiet Game. Uncle Brewster wanted to know whether they were Gamblers or Business Men, and the Boy said they were Business Men. It was all Friendly, with an Ante of Two Bits and the Chandelier as the Limit. Uncle Brewster said he was accustomed to playing with Lima Beans, Three for a Cent and One call Two and no fair to Bluff. The Bell-Hopper told him to Turn In and get a Good Night's Rest.

Next Morning at the Hotel he spotted a stylish little Chunk of a Woman who kept the Cigar Case and sold Books with Actress Photos on the outside.

He walked over to buy a Cigar, but he happened to see the "3 for 50c." Label and his Feet got cold.

So, instead of buying a Cigar, he conversed with the Proprietress. He seemed to be a Success with her, and ventured to say that he was a Stranger in Town and would like first-rate to go out to a Lecture or some other kind of Entertainment that Evening if he could find a Nice Girl that didn't mind going with a Respectable Man who could give References, and besides was nearly old enough to be her Father. Then after the Lecture they could go to a First-Class Restaurant and have an Oyster Stew.

Uncle Brewster had read the Illustrated Papers in the Barber Shop out Home, and he certainly knew what was Expected of a Man who wanted to give a Gay Girl the Time of her Life.

The Cigar and Literary Girl said she would be Charmed to Accompany him only for one Thing: She said she didn't have a Hat that was Fit to Wear. She said she could tell by his Looks that he was a Gentleman that wouldn't want to go anywhere with a Lady whose Lid was Tacky. Possibly he would be willing to Stake her to a Hat.

"What would the Hat come to?" asked Uncle Brewster, somewhat Leary.

"Only Fourteen Dollars," she replied.

"I'll Think it Over," quoth Uncle Brewster, in a choking Voice, and he was so Groggy he walked into the Elevator instead of going out the Street Door.

A little while later Uncle Brewster met an Acquaintance who gave him a Complimentary Badge to the Races. He walked out to the Track, so as to make the Expense as Reasonable as possible.

As soon as he was in the Ring a Tout took him back of a Hot Sausage Booth and told him not to Give it Out, but Green Pill in the First Race was sure to Win as far as a man could throw an Anvil, and to hurry and get a Piece of Money on. Uncle

UNCLE BREWSTER

Brewster looked at the Entries and began to Quiver. He wished that Doc Jimmison could be there to Advise him. Green Pill was 30 to 1, and the Tout had his information from a Stable Boy that slept with the Horse.

A Reckless Spirit seized Uncle Brewster. He said he would take a Chance even if he didn't know for Sure that he would Win. So he walked up to a Bookie and said to him: "I want to Bet Fifty Cents on Green Pill, and this is a Dollar here, so you want to give me Fifty Cents Change."

THE INVITATION

Whereupon the Bookie told him to Back Up and Fade and do a Disappearing Specialty.

Uncle Brewster Escaped and found himself at a Bar. He decided that he would take a Drink, because he wouldn't be Home until next Day and by that time it would be off his Breath.

So he laid his Bosom against the Brass Railing and said to the Man in White, "You might as well draw me a Glass of Beer."

"We've got it in Bottles," said the Barkeeper, regarding Uncle Brewster without a sign of Enthusiasm.

NON-COMBUSTIBLE

"What do you git for a Bottle?" asked Uncle Brewster.

"Twenty Cents," was the Reply of the Liquor Clerk.

"Keep it," said Uncle Brewster.

Perceiving that the Race-Track was in the hands of Gougers, Uncle Brewster walked back to the Hotel. By that Time his New Shoes had Crippled him, and he decided to take the Afternoon Train for home instead of Waiting Over.

That Evening he was back at his own Fireside, with the Bunged-Up Feet resting in Carpet Slippers. As he sat and read the Poultry Magazine, Aunt Mehely looked at him sidewise, and full of Suspicion said, "I s'pose you just Played Hob there in the City."

And Uncle Brewster replied as follows: "No, Mother, I didn't Drink and I didn't Gamble. I didn't do Nothin'—not even go to a Theayter."

And as he spoke an Aureole of Virtue seemed to curdle above him, while his Countenance bore an Expression of Placid Triumph, which meant that he was the real Asbestos Paragon who had been tried in the Furnace and declared Non-Combustible.

MORAL: *Some People are Good because it Comes High to be Otherwise.*

THE FABLE *OF THE* GRASS WIDOW *AND* THE MESMEREE *AND THE* SIX DOLLARS

ONE Day a keen Business manager who thought nobody could Show him was sitting at his Desk. A Grass Widow floated in, and stood Smiling at him. She was a Blonde, and had a Gown that fit her as if she had been Packed into it by Hydraulic Pressure. She was just as Demure as Edna May ever tried to be, but the Business Manager was a Lightning Calculator, and he Surmised that the Bunk was about to be Handed to him. The Cold Chills went down his Spine when he caught a Flash of the Half-Morocco Prospectus.

If it had been a Man Agent he would have shouted "Sick 'em" and reached for a Paper-Weight. But when the Agent has the Venus de Milo beaten on Points and Style, and when the Way the Skirt sets isn't so Poor, and she is Coy and introduces the Startled Fawn way of backing up without getting any farther away, and when she comes on with short Steps, and he gets the remote Swish of the Real Silk, to say nothing of the Faint Aroma of New-Mown Hay, and her Hesitating Manner seems to ask, "Have I or have I not met a Friend?"—in a Case of that kind, the Victim is just the same as Strapped to the Operating-Table. He has about One Chance in a Million.

The timorous but trusting little Grass Widow sat beside the Business Manager and told him her Hard-Luck Story in low, bird-like Notes. She said she was the only Support of her Little Boy, who was attending a Military School at Syracuse, N. Y. She turned the Liquid Orbs on him and had him to the Bad. He thought he would tell her that already he had more Books at Home than he could get on the Shelves, but when he tried to Talk he only Yammered. She Kept on with her little Song, and Smiled all the Time, and sat a little Closer, and he got so Dizzy he had to lock his Legs under the Office Chair to keep from Sinking Away.

When she had him in the Hypnotic State she pushed the Silver Pencil into his Right Hand, and showed him where to sign his

Name. He wrote it, while the dim Sub-Consciousness told him that probably he was the Softest Thing the Lady Robber had Stood Up that Season. Then she recovered the Pencil, which he was confusedly trying to put into his Vest Pocket, and missing it about Six Inches, and with a cheery Good By she was gone.

He shook himself and took a Long Breath, and asked where he was. Then it all came back to him and he felt Ornery, and called

GRASS WIDOW

himself Names and roasted the Office Boy in the Next Room,
and made a Rule that hereafter Nobody could get at him except
by Card, and if any Blonde Sharks in Expensive Costumes asked
for him, to call up the Chief and ask for a Squad.

He was so Wrothy at himself for being Held Up that he could
not find any Consolation except in the Fact that he had seen on
the List of Subscribers the name of nearly every well-known

THE OFFICE BOY

married Citizen above the Age of 35. He was not the Only One. She had Corralled the Street.

When the Man came around to deliver the seven-pound copy of "Happy Hours with the Poets," and he paid out his Six Silver Pieces for a queer Volume that he would not have Read for Six an Hour, he hated himself worse than ever. He thought some of giving the Book to the Office Boy, by way of Revenge, but he hit upon a Better Use for it. He put it back into the Box and carried it Home, and said to his Wife, "See what I have Bought for you."

It occurred to him that after getting a Present like that, she ought to let him stay out every Night for a Month. But she could not see it that Way. He had to tell her that Some Women never seem to Appreciate having Husbands to Grind and Toil all day, so as to be able to purchase Beautiful Gifts for them. Then she told him that all the Women of her Acquaintance had received these Books as Presents, and a crowd of Married Men must have been given a Club Rate. Then he Spunked up and said that if she was going to look a Gift Horse in the Mouth, they wouldn't Talk about it any more.

In the meantime the Grass Widow was living at the Waldorf-Astoria.

MORAL: *Those who are Entitled to it Get it sooner or later.*

THE FABLE *OF THE* HONEST MONEY-MAKER AND THE PARTNER OF HIS JOYS, *SUCH AS THEY WERE*

THE Prosperous Farmer lived in an Agricultural Section of the Middle West. He commanded the Respect of all his Neighbors. He owned a Section, and had a Raft of big Horses and white-faced Cows and Farm Machinery, and Money in the Bank besides. He still had the first Dollar he ever made, and it could not have been taken away from him with Pincers.

Henry was a ponderous, Clydesdale kind of Man, with Warts on his Hands. He did not have to travel on Appearances, because the whole County knew what he was Worth. Of course he was Married. Years before he had selected a willing Country Girl with Pink Cheeks, and put her into his Kitchen to serve the Remainder of her Natural Life. He let her have as high as Two Dollars a Year to spend for herself. Her Hours were from 6 A. M. to 6 A. M., and if she got any Sleep she had to take it out of her Time. The Eight-Hour Day was not recognized on Henry's Place.

After Ten Years of raising Children, Steaming over the Washtub, Milking the Cows, Carrying in Wood, Cooking for the Hands, and other Delsarte such as the Respected Farmer usually Frames Up for his Wife, she was as thin as a Rail and humped over in the Shoulders. She was Thirty, and looked Sixty. Her Complexion was like Parchment and her Voice had been worn to a Cackle. She was losing her Teeth, too, but Henry could not afford to pay Dentist Bills because he needed all his Money to buy more Poland Chinas and build other Cribs. If she wanted a Summer Kitchen or a new Wringer or a Sewing Machine, or Anything Else that would lighten her Labors, Henry would Moan and Grumble and say she was trying to land him in the Poorhouse.

They had a dandy big Barn, painted Red with White Trimmings, and a Patent Fork to lift the Hay into the Mow, and the Family lived in a Pine Box that had not been Painted in Years and had Dog-Fennel all around the Front of it.

The Wife of the Respected Farmer was the only Work Animal around the Place that was not kept Fat and Sleek. But, of course, Henry did not count on Selling her. Henry often would fix up his Blooded Stock for the County Fair and tie Blue Ribbons on the Percherons and Herefords, but it was never noticed that he tied any Blue Ribbons on the Wife.

HENRY

And yet Henry was a Man to be Proud of. He never Drank and he was a Good Hand with Horses, and he used to go to Church on Sunday Morning and hold a Cud of Tobacco in his Face during Services and sing Hymns with Extreme Unction. He would sing that he was a Lamb and had put on the Snow-White Robes and that Peace attended him. People would see him there in his Store Suit, with the Emaciated Wife and the Scared Children

THE FARM

sitting in the Shadow of his Greatness, and they said that she was Lucky to have a Man who was so Well Off and lived in the Fear of the Lord.

Henry was Patriotic as well as Pious. He had a Picture of Abraham Lincoln in the Front Room, which no one was permitted to Enter, and he was glad that Slavery had been abolished.

Henry robbed the Cradle in order to get Farm-Hands. As soon as the Children were able to Walk without holding on, he started them for the Corn-Field, and told them to Pay for the Board that they had been Sponging off of him up to that Time. He did not want them to get too much Schooling for fear that they would want to sit up at Night and Read instead of Turning In so as to get an Early Start along before Daylight next Morning. So they did not get any too much, rest easy. And he never Foundered them on Stick Candy or Raisins or any such Delicatessen for sale at a General Store. Henry was undoubtedly the Tightest Wad in the Township. Some of the Folks who had got into a Box through Poor Management, and had been Foreclosed out of House and Home by Henry and his Lawyer, used to say that Henry was a Skin, and was too Stingy to give his Family enough to Eat, but most People looked up to Henry, for there was no getting around it that he was Successful.

When the Respected Farmer had been Married for Twenty Years and the Children had developed into long Gawks who did not know Anything except to get out and Toil all Day for Pa and not be paid anything for it, and after Henry had scraped together more Money than you could load on a Hay-Rack, an Unfortunate Thing happened. His Wife began to Fail. She was now Forty, but the Fair and Fat did not go with it. At that Age some Women are Buxom and just blossoming into the Full Charm of Matronly Womanhood. But Henry's Wife was Gaunt and Homely and all Run Down. She had been Poorly for Years, but she had to keep up and do the Chores as well as the House-Work, because Henry could not afford to hire a Girl. At last her Back gave out, so that she had to sit down and Rest every Once in a While. Henry would come in for his Meals and to let her know how Hearty all the Calves seemed to be, and he began to Notice that she was not very Chipper. It worried him more than a little, because he did

not care to pay any Doctor Bills. He told her she had better go
and get some Patent Medicine that he had seen advertised on
the Fence coming out from Town. It was only Twenty-Five cents
a Bottle, and was warranted to Cure Anything. So she tried it,
but it did not seem to restore her Youth and she got Weaker,
and at last Henry just had to have the Doctor, Expense or No

THE FAMILY

Expense. The Doctor said that as nearly as he could Diagnose her Case, she seemed to be Worn Out. Henry was Surprised, and said she had not been Complaining any more than Usual.

Next Afternoon he was out Dickering for a Bull, and his Woman lying on the cheap Bedstead, up under the hot Roof, folded her lean Hands and slipped away to the only Rest she had known since she tied up with a Prosperous and Respected Farmer.

Henry was all Broken Up. He Wailed and Sobbed and made an Awful Fuss at the Church.The Preacher tried to Comfort him by saying that the Ways of Providence were beyond all Finding Out. He said that probably there was some Reason why the Sister had been taken right in the Prime of her Usefulness, but it was not for Henry to know it. He said the only Consolation he could offer was the Hope that possibly she was Better Off. There did not seem to be much Doubt about that.

In about a Month the Respected Farmer was riding around the Country in his Buck-Board looking for Number Two. He had a business Head and he knew it was Cheaper to Marry than to Hire one. His Daughter was only Eleven and not quite Big Enough as yet to do all the Work for five Men.

Finally he found one who had the Reputation of being a Good Worker. When he took her over to his House to Break Her In, the Paper at the County Seat referred to them as the Happy Couple.

MORAL: *Be Honest and Respected and it Goes.*

THE FABLE OF WHY SWEETIE FLEW THE TRACK

ONCE there were two Married People who used "Lovey" and "Pet" when they were in Company, and as soon as they were at Home they Threw Things at each other. She used to watch him through a Hole in the Curtain to see if he Flirted with any Women as he walked up the Street, and he bribed the Hired Girl to tell him Everything that happened while he was off the Reservation.

They did not Mocha and Java worth a Cent.

The Cardboard Motto in the Dining Room said, "Love One Another," but they were too Busy to Read.

He had a Clearing on the top of his Head and wore Side-Whiskers and bore a general Resemblance to the Before in an Ad for a Facial Treatment, and yet she suspected that all the Women in Town were Crazy to steal him away from her.

Likewise, inasmuch as she was the same Width all the way up and down, the same as a Poster Girl, and used to sport a Velvet Shroud with Black Beads on it, and could wield a Tooth-Pick and carry on a Conversation at the same time, he knew that sooner or later some Handsome Wretch with Money would try to Abduct her.

Sometimes he would bring a Friend Home to Dinner, and then if the Friend extended himself and told the Missus how well she was looking or Perjured himself over her Hand-Painting, Papa would get a Grouch and hide in the Corner.

Then she would Fan herself rapidly and ask, "Aren't you well, Dear?"

Dear would force one of those Dying-Martyr Smiles and reply, "I am quite well, Puss."

Then Puss would tell the Visitor that Baby was simply ruining his Health through Devotion to his Employers, but they didn't seem to Appreciate him at all.

After the Visitor went away there would be Language all over the Shop, and the poor Hired Girl would lock the Door and write to the Intelligence Office for a new Place.

Truly, it was a Happy Little Home, with the Reverse English.

She would Frisk his Wardrobe every day or two, looking for Evidence, and he would compel her to Itemize her Accounts so that he might be sure she was not giving Jewelry to the Iceman.

She would find a certain Passage in a Book, relating to Man's Cruelty and Woman's Silent Suffering, and then she would Mark the Passage and put it where he could Find it. Then when he Found it, he would Mark it "Rot!" and put it where She could find it, and then she would Weep and write Letters to Lady Authors telling them how Sad and Lonely she was.

But all the Time they kept up an Affectionate Front before their Acquaintances. They thought it better to avoid Scenes in Public; and although each knew that the other was False and had ceased to Love, they could not bring themselves to think of a Separation or a Divorce on account of the Cat—their Cat! The cat must never know.

However, one of his Business Associates was On. He was a Bachelor and had lived at a European Hotel for Years, and he knew just how to Arbitrate a Domestic Scrap. So he sat down one day and gave the Husband a Good Talking-To. He said it was a Shame that such Nice People should have their Differences when it was so easy to be Happy. With that he handed over a Slew of Platitudes and Proverbs, such as: "A Soft Answer Turneth Away Wrath," "It takes Two to Make a Quarrel," "Think Twice before you Speak once," *et cetera*.

The Gist of his heart-to-heart Talk was that any Husband could stop Rough House Proceedings and shoot all kinds of Sweetness and Light into the sassiest Mooch a Wife ever got on to herself, if only he would refuse to Quarrel with her, receive her Flings without a Show of Wrath, and get up every Morning ready to Plug for a Renaissance of their Early Love.

Oh, but it was a Beauty Bright System! The European Hotel Bachelor said it couldn't Lose.

The Husband decided to give it a Trial. That very Afternoon he met his Wife, who had come out in her long Fawn-Colored Coat that fell straight in the Back. She had her Upper Rigging set, and was trying to Blanket everything on the Street. He flashed a Smiling Countenance, and said he was glad to see her.

Then, instead of asking her When she left the House, and Where she had been since then, and How Soon she expected to go Home again, he told her she was looking Unusually Charming. She was Startled.

He handed her a Ten and told her to have a Good Time. Now, usually, when she wanted any Pin Money, she had to Pry it out of him.

On her way home her Mind was in a Tumult. Why had he given her the Con Speech and all that Money? What was the Ulterior

BABY

Motive? What had he been Doing that he should attempt to
Coddle her into a Forgiving Mood? Did he Fear that she would
get next to his Past? Huh?

He just couldn't Fool her. She knew Something was Doing.
Else why should he try to Fix her?

As soon as he came Home that Evening she Accused him and
said she knew All. Instead of Countering with the usual Gibe,
he told her that she was the Only Woman he had ever Loved and
would she go to a Show that Evening? She went, thinking that

SWEETIE

perhaps the Other Woman might be there and she could detect some Signal passing between them. While at the Theater he fanned her and explained the Plot, and was all Attention. They rode Home in a Cab, because he said a Car wasn't good enough for His Queen. After they were at Home he asked her to sing the Song he had liked so much in the Old Days, "My Bonnie Lies Over the Ocean." This was Conclusive Proof to her that the Hussy's Name was Bonnie.

Next Morning before he started away he Kissed her, and it

THE CAT

wasn't any Make-Believe such as you see in Comic Opera. It was a genuine Olga Nethersole Buss, full of Linger and Adhesion. To cap the Climax he said he would stop in and order some Violets.

As soon as the Door slammed she Staggered toward the Kitchen, holding on to the Furniture here and there, the same as a Sardou Heroine. In the Kitchen was a Box of Rough on Rats. Hastily Concealing it beneath the loose Folds of her Morning Gown, she went to her Room and looked in the Mirror.

Ah, when he saw that Cold, White Face, then he would be Sorry. Upon Second Thought, this didn't seem to be a Moral Certainty, so she Weakened and had the Girl take the Poison and Hide it. She said she would Live—Live to Forget his Perfidy.

That day she went back to Mamma, and took the Cat with her.

When he came Home in the Twilight he found no Wife, no Cat—only a Scribbled Note saying that he could no longer Deceive her; that she had seen through his Diabolical Plan to Lull her Suspicions, and that she was no longer Safe in the Same House.

When the Deserted Husband went to the Friend and told him what had Happened, the Wise Bachelor said:

"I see. You did not go at her Strong enough."

MORAL: *They don't know Anything about it.*

THE FABLE *OF THE* EX-CHATTEL *AND THE* AWFUL SWAT *THAT* WAS WAITING *FOR THE* COLONEL

IN one of the States of the Sunny South there stood a war-time House that had six white Columns along the Veranda, and the Chimney ran up the outside of the Wall.

This House was the Abode of a Colonel who had a silver-gray Goatee and the Manners of the Old School. All the First Families in the State were related to him, and therefore he was somewhat Particular as to who Lined Up with him when he took his Toddy.

He was proud of his Ancestry, and he carried the Scars to prove that he would Resent an Insult.

Now it happened that the Thirteenth Amendment signified nothing to him. He had been Reconstructed, but it didn't Take.

While on a Business Trip to the North he stopped at a Gaudy Hotel with all kinds of Mirrors and Onyx Stairways.

The Head Waiter at this Hotel was a Colored Gentleman with a False Front and a Dress Suit that fit him too soon. His Name was Mr. Winfield. He was President of the Colored Waiters' Union, Vice-President of the Republican County Central Committee, and Regal Commander of the Princes of Ethiopia.

His Honors lay Heavily upon him. He showed People where to sit in the Dining Room, and those who failed to Obey usually had to wait fifteen or twenty Minutes for their Vermicelli.

Mr. Winfield favored his Feet somewhat, which caused him to walk Syncopated, but, everything considered, he was quite Important and fairly Warm.

One morning the Colonel went into the Dining Room, and after he had seated himself he called Mr. Winfield to him and said he wanted some Hot Biscuit. At the same time he addressed Mr. Winfield as a Black Hound. Mr. Winfield did not know that this was a Term of Endearment in Apahatchie County, so he picked up a Silver Fruit Dish and bounced it against the Colonel's Head.

The Colonel arose and pulled his Persuader, expecting to make it a Case of Justifiable Homicide, but two Waiters named George and Grant grabbed him and backed him up against the Wall.

There were other guests in the Dining Room, but they did not jump in with any Gun Plays and make it a Race War, because Apahatchie County was Eight Hundred Miles away. One of them Co-Operated to the extent of Ringing three times for a Policeman.

The Officer of the Law who arrived in a few Minutes was Mr. Otis Beasley, Most Worshipful Scribe of the Princes of Ethiopia, of which Mr. Winfield was the Regal Commander.

Mr. Beasley walked up to Mr. Winfield, and placing his Left Hand on his Brow, said, "Hail, Brother."

"Hail, Most Noble Prince!" responded Mr. Winfield, making the Mystic Sign.

"What are the Objects of our Beloved Fraternity?" asked Mr. Beasley, in a whisper.

"Hope, Coslosterousness, and Polotomy," replied the Regal Commander.

"'Tis Well," said the Most Worshipful Scribe, giving him the Grip.

Having completed the Secret work, Mr. Beasley wanted to know what he could do for Brother Winfield.

"Remove this Pusson," said Mr. Winfield, pointing at the Colonel.

So it came about that He who in Apahatchie County had trained them to hop off the Sidewalk and stand Uncovered until he had passed, now suffered the Hideous Degradation of being marched downstairs by One of Them and then slammed into the Hurry-Up Wagon. Under which Circumstances the Colonel had the Rabies.

At the Police Station he was dragged before a Magistrate and was charged with Disorderly Conduct, Carrying Concealed Weapons, Assault and Battery, Assault with Intent to Kill, and Resisting an Officer.

The Magistrate was a White Man, and to him the Colonel appealed for Justice, claiming Brotherhood as a Caucasian. He told what would have happened in Apahatchie if any Coon had dared to lay a finger on a Colonel.

Here was an opening for the Court. It must be known that the Court lived in a Ward that was Dark in one End, and he was out for the Colored Vote in case he ran for Judge. This was his Chance to make a Grand-Stand Play.

He handed down a Decision to the Effect that all Men are Free and Equal, with incidental References to the Emancipation Proclamation and Striking the Shackles from Four Millions of Human Beings. He Ratified the Constitution and Permitted the Negro to stand in the Free Sunlight. In Apahatchie County he

THE COLONEL

would have been used for Target Practice, but Apahatchie
County was still Eight Hundred Miles away.

In Conclusion he Soaked the Colonel for $32.75 in Fines and
Costs, Confiscating the Weapon, which he afterward presented
to Officer Otis Beasley as a Slight Token of Esteem.

Next Morning, as a south-bound Passenger Train was crossing
the Ohio River, the Colored Porter on the Atlanta Sleeper jumped
eighty feet from the Trestle into the Water in order to Escape with
his Life.

MORAL: *A Head Waiter must be Ruled by Kindness.*

MR. WINFIELD

THE FABLE *OF* WHAT HAPPENED *THE* NIGHT THE MEN CAME *TO THE* WOMEN'S CLUB

IN a Progressive Little City claiming about twice the Population that the Census Enumerators could uncover, there was a Literary Club. It was one of these Clubs guaranteed to fix you out with Culture while you wait. Two or three Matrons, who were too Heavy for Light Amusements, but not old enough to remain at Home and Knit, organized the Club. Nearly every Woman in town rushed to get in, for fear somebody would say she hadn't been Asked.

The Club used to Round Up once a week at the Homes of Members. There would be a Paper, followed by a Discussion, after which somebody would Pour.

The Organization seemed to be a Winner. One Thing the Lady Clubbers were Dead Set On. They were going to have Harmony with an Upper Case H. They were out to cut a seven-foot Swath through English Literature from Beowulf to Bangs, inclusive, and no petty Jealousies or Bickerings would stand in the Way.

So while they were at the Club they would pull Kittenish Smiles at each other, and Applaud so as not to split the Gloves. Some times they would Kiss, too, but they always kept their Fingers crossed.

Of course, when they got off in Twos and Threes they would pull the little Meat-Axes out of the Reticules and hack a few Monograms, but that was to have been expected.

Everything considered, the Club was a Tremendous Go. At each Session the Lady President would announce the Subject for the next Meeting. For instance, she would say that Next Week they would take up Wyclif. Then every one would romp home to look in the Encyclopedia of Authors and find out who in the world Wyclif was. On the following Thursday they would have Wyclif down Pat, and be primed for a Discussion. They would talk about Wyclif as if he had been down to the House for Tea every evening that Week.

After the Club had been running for Six Months it was beginning to be Strong on Quotations and Dates. The Members knew that Mrs. Browning was the wife of Mr. Browning, that Milton had Trouble with his Eyes, and that Lord Byron wasn't all that he should have been, to say the Least. They began to feel their Intellectual Oats. In the meantime the Jeweler's Wife had designed a Club Badge.

The Club was doing such Notable Work that some of the Members thought they ought to have a Special Meeting and invite the Men. They wanted to put the Cap-Sheaf on a Profitable Season, and at the same time hand the Merited Rebuke to some of the Husbands and Brothers who had been making Funny Cracks.

It was decided to give the Star Programme at the Beadle Home, and after the Papers had been read then all the Men and Five Women who did not hold office could file through the Front Room and shake Hands with the President, the Vice-President, the Recording Secretary, the Corresponding Secretary, the Treasurer, and the members of the various Committees, all of whom were to line up and Receive.

The reason the Club decided to have the Brain Barbecue at the Beadle Home was that the Beadles had such beautiful big Rooms and Double Doors. There was more or less quiet Harpoon Work when the Announcement was made. Several of the Elderly Ones said that Josephine Beadle was not a Representative Member of the Club. She was Fair to look upon, but she was not pulling very hard for the Uplifting of the Sex. It was suspected that she came to the Meetings just to Kill Time and see what the Others were Wearing. She refused to buckle down to Literary Work, for she was a good deal more interested in the Bachelors who filled the Windows of the new Men's Club than she was in the Butler who wrote "Hudibras." So why should she have the Honor of entertaining the Club at the Annual Meeting? Unfortunately, the Members who had the most Doing under their Bonnets were not the ones who could come to the Front with large Rooms that could be Thrown together, so the Beadle Home got the Great Event.

Every one in Town who carried a Pound of Social Influence

showed up in his or her Other Clothes. Extra Chairs had to be
brought in, and what with the Smilax and Club Colors it was
very Swell, and the Maiden in the Lace Mitts who was going to
write about it for the Weekly threw a couple of Spasms.

The Men were led in pulling at the Halters and with their Ears
laid back. After they got into the Dressing Room they Stuck
there until they had to be Shooed out. They did not know what
they were going against, but they had their Suspicions. They

WYCLIF

managed to get Rear Seats or stand along the Wall so that they could execute the Quiet Sneak if Things got too Literary. The Women were too Flushed and Proud to Notice.

At 8:30 P. M. the Lady President stood out and began to read a few Pink Thoughts on "Woman's Destiny—Why Not?" Along toward 9:15, about the time the Lady President was beginning to show up Good and Earnest, Josephine Beadle, who was Circulating around on the Outskirts of the Throng to make sure that everybody was Happy, made a Discovery. She noticed that the Men standing along the Wall and in the Doorways were not more than sixty per cent En Rapport with the Long Piece about Woman's Destiny. Now Josephine was right there to see that Everybody had a Nice Time, and she did not like to see the Prominent Business Men of the Town dying of Thirst or Leg Cramp or anything like that, so she gave two or three of them the Quiet Wink, and they tiptoed after her out to the Dining Room, where she offered Refreshments, and said they could slip out on the Side Porch and Smoke if they wanted to.

Probably they preferred to go back in the Front Room and hear some more about Woman's Destiny not.

As soon as they could master their Emotions and get control of their Voices, they told Josephine what they thought of her. They said she made the Good Samaritan look like a Cheap Criminal, and if she would only say the Word they would begin to put Ground Glass into the Food at Home. Then Josephine called them "Boys," which probably does not make a Hit with one who is on the sloping side of 48. More of the Men seemed to awake to the Fact that they were Overlooking something, so they came on the Velvet Foot back to the Dining Room and declared themselves In, and flocked around Josephine and called her "Josie" and "Joe." They didn't care. They were having a Pleasant Visit.

Josephine gave them Allopathic Slugs of the Size that they feed you in the Navy and then lower you into the Dingey and send you Ashore. Then she let them go out on the Porch to smoke. By the time the Lady President came to the last Page there were only two Men left in the Front Room. One was Asleep and the other was Penned In.

The Women were Huffy. They went out to make the Men come in, and found them Bunched on the Porch listening to a Story that a Traveling Man had just brought to Town that Day.

Now the Plan was that during the Reception the Company would stand about in little Groups, and ask each other what Books they liked, and make it something on the order of a Salon. This Plan miscarried, because all the Men wanted to hear Rag Time played by Josephine, the Life-Saver. Josephine had to yield,

THE MEN

and the Men all clustered around her to give their Moral Support. After one or two Selections, they felt sufficiently Keyed to begin to hit up those low-down Songs about Baby and Chickens and Razors. No one paid any Attention to the Lady President, who was off in a Corner holding an Indignation Meeting with the Secretary and the Vice-President.

When the Women began to sort out the Men and order them to start Home and all the Officers of the Club were giving Josephine the frosty Good Night, any one could see that there was Trouble ahead.

Next Day the Club held a Special Session and expelled Josephine for Conduct Unbecoming a Member, and Josephine sent Word to them as follows: "Rats."

Then the Men quietly got together and bought Josephine about a Thousand Dollars' Worth of American Beauty Roses to show that they were With her, and then Homes began to break up, and somebody started the Report that anyway it was the Lady President's Fault for having such a long and pokey Essay that wasn't hers at all, but had been Copied out of a Club Paper published in Detroit.

Before the next Meeting there were two Factions. The Lady President had gone to a Rest Cure, and the Meeting resolved itself into a Good Cry and a general Smash-Up.

MORAL: *The only Literary Men are those who have to Work at it.*

THE MAGNATE

THE FABLE OF THE CORPORATION DIRECTOR AND THE MISLAID AMBITION

ONE of the Most Promising Boys in a Graded School had a Burning Ambition to be a Congressman. He loved Politics and Oratory. When there was a Rally in Town he would carry a Torch and listen to the Spellbinder with his Mouth open.

The Boy wanted to grow up and wear a Black String Tie and a Bill Cody Hat and walk stiff-legged, with his Vest unbuttoned at the Top, and be Distinguished.

On Friday Afternoons he would go to School with his Face scrubbed to a shiny pink and his Hair roached up on one side, and he would Recite the Speeches of Patrick Henry and Daniel Webster and make Gestures.

When he Graduated from the High School he delivered an Oration on "The Duty of the Hour," calling on all young Patriots to leap into the Arena and with the Shield of Virtue quench the rising Flood of Corruption. He said that the Curse of Our Times was the Greed for Wealth, and he pleaded for Unselfish Patriotism among those in High Places.

He boarded at Home for a while without seeing a chance to jump into the Arena, and finally his Father worked a Pull and got him a Job with a Steel Company. He proved to be a Handy Young Man, and the Manger sent Him out to make Contracts. He stopped roaching his Hair, and he didn't give the Arena of Politics any serious Consideration except when the Tariff on Steel was in Danger.

In a little while he owned a few Shares, and after that he became a Director. He joined several Clubs and began to enjoy his Food. He drank a Small Bottle with his Luncheon each Day, and he couldn't talk Business unless he held a Scotch High Ball in his Right Hand.

With the return of Prosperity and the Formation of the Trust and the Whoop in all Stocks he made so much Money that he was afraid to tell the Amount.

His Girth increased—he became puffy under the Eyes—you could see the little blue Veins on his Nose.

He kept his Name out of the Papers as much as possible, and he never gave Congress a Thought except when he talked to his

AMBITIOUS YOUTH

Lawyer of the Probable Manner in which they would Evade
any Legislation against Trusts. He took two Turkish Baths every
week and wore Silk Underwear. When an Eminent Politician
would come to his Office to shake him down he would send out
Word by the Boy in Buttons that he had gone to Europe. That's
what he thought of Politics.

One day while rummaging in a lower Drawer in his Library,
looking for a Box of Poker Chips, he came upon a Roll of Manuscript and wondered what it was. He opened it and read how it
was the Duty of all True Americans to hop into the Arena and
struggle unselfishly for the General Good. It came to him in a
Flash—this was his High School Oration!

Then suddenly he remembered that for several Years of his
Life his consuming Ambition had been—to go to Congress!

With a demoniacal Shriek he threw himself at full length on a
Leather Couch and began to Laugh.

He rolled off the Sofa and tossed about on a $1,200 Rug in a
Paroxysm of Merriment.

His Man came running into the Library and saw the Master
in Convulsions. The poor Trust Magnate was purple in the Face.

They sent for a Great Specialist, who said that his Dear Friend
had ruptured one of the smaller Arteries, and also narrowly
escaped Death by Apoplexy.

He advised Rest and Quiet and the avoidance of any Great
Shock.

So they took the High School Oration and put it on the Ice,
and the Magnate slowly recovered and returned to his nine-
course Dinners.

MORAL: *Of all Sad Words of Tongue or Pen, the Saddest are
these, "It Might Have Been."*

LADY PRESIDENT

THE FABLE *OF* WHY ESSIE'S TALL FRIEND GOT *THE* FRESH AIR

THE Owner of a Furnishing Store gave employment to a Boy with Dreamy Eyes, who took good care of his Nails and used Scented Soap and carried a Pocket Looking-Glass. It was his Delight to stand in the Doorway and watch the Girls all Color Up when they caught Sight of him. He was said to be a Divine Waltzer at these Balls that cost the Gents 50 cents each and the Ladies get in free.

There was a Girl named Essie who was Hanging Around the Front of the Store about half of the Time, waiting to get a chance to Speak to Bert. She Chewed Gum and kept her Sailor Hat pulled down to her Eyebrows and had her Name worked out in Wire and used it as a Breastpin. After she had waited an Hour or so, and he had Broken Away long enough to take her aside, she would want to know what it was that Net had said about her, or else she would ask why he had not Answered her Note. It was always just about as Momentous as that.

If Essie did not come, she sent some one with a Message, and sometimes other Floor Managers with Red Neckties and Forelocks would come in to see about the Arrangements for the next Grand Hop by the Eucalyptus Pleasure Club.

Bert was so Engrossed with his Love Affairs and the Pleasure Club and the Bundle of Correspondence that he carried with him that he had little Time for Furnishing Goods. It used to Annoy him considerably when any one came in and wanted to Spend Money. He would set out the Goods in a Manner that showed it to be something of a Come-Down for him to be compelled to Wait on Outsiders. While the Customer would be asking Questions, Bert would be working the Flexible Neck to see if Essie was still waiting for him. Sometimes when there was a Rush he would get real Cross, and if People did not Buy in a Hurry he would slam the Boxes around and be Lippy and give them the Eye. Yet he wondered why he did not get a Raise in Salary.

During the Holiday Season, when the Eucalyptus Pleasure

Club was simply in a Delirium of All-Night Dances and Fried-Oyster Suppers, and when Essie had worn a Path in the Snow coming down to tell Bert not to Forget, the Proprietor decided that the Boy's Job was interfering with his Gaiety. So when Bert came to get his Envelope the Furnisher told him he needed more Outdoor Life and Exercise, and he had better find it by moving around Town and looking for another Job.

MORAL: *Omit the Essie Proposition.*

ESSIE

THE FABLE OF THE MICHIGAN COUNTER-FEIT WHO WASN'T ONE THING OR THE OTHER

TWO Travelers sat in a Sleeping Car that was fixed up with Plush and Curly-Cues until it resembled a Chambermaid's Dream of Paradise. They were talking about the Man who sat across the Aisle.

"I think he is an Englishman," said the First Traveler.

"Why do you think so?" queried his Companion.

"Well, in the first place his Clothes don't fit him," replied the First Traveler. "I observe, also, that he has piled all his Luggage on Another Man's Seat, that he has opened several Windows without asking Permission, that he has expected the Porter to pay Attention to him and nobody else, and that he has Kicked at something every Thirty Seconds since we left Buffalo."

"You make out a Strong Case," said the Second Traveler, nodding. "I will admit that the Suit is Fierce. Still, I maintain that he is not an Englishman. I notice that he seems somewhat Ashamed of his Clothes. Now, if he were an Englishman, he would Glory in the Misfit."

"Perhaps he is a Canadian," suggested the First Traveler.

"Impossible," said the other. "He may be English, but he is not sufficiently British to be a Canadian. If he were a Canadian he would now be singing 'Britannia Rules the Wave!' No, I insist that he is an American traveling Incog. I suspect that I have Caught him with the Goods. While sitting here, I have had my Sherlock Holmes System at work. A few Moments ago he read a Joke in a Comic Paper, and the Light of Appreciation kindled in his Eye before a full Minute had elapsed."

"Perhaps it was not a Comic Paper at all," said the First Traveler. "It may have been Punch. Very often an Englishman will Get Next almost immediately if the Explanation is put in Parenthesis. You have to Hand it to him with a Diagram and a Map and then give him a little Time, and then he Drops. This man is certainly an Englishman. Notice the Expression of Disapproval. He does not fancy our Farm Scenery. Get onto the Shoes, too. They are shaped like Muffins. Then if you are still in Doubt, pay attention to the Accent. Didn't you hear him just now when he was complaining to the Porter because the Sun was on the wrong side of the Car?"

"Yes, but did you hear him use 'Cahn't' and 'Glass' both in the same Sentence? When a Man Plays it Both Ways, it is a Sign

PULLMAN CAR

that he was born in Wisconsin and attended Harvard. I am convinced that he is not an Englishman at all. He is probably an American who takes a Bahth in a Bath-Tub."

But the First Traveler persisted that surely the Man across the aisle was an Englishman, so they Jawed back and forth and finally made a Bet. Then the First Traveler stepped over and begged the Stranger's Pardon and asked him, as a personal favor, to Identify himself. Was he an Englishman or an American?

"Really, that is a Hard Question to answer," said the Surprised Stranger. "I confess with some Mortification that Father was an American, but he wore Detachable Cuffs and talked about Live Stock at the Table, so the Heirs are trying to Forget him. As nearly as we can learn, one of my Ancestors came to this Country from Yorkshire early in the Eighteenth Century and founded a Tannery in Massachusetts, so I feel that I can claim an English Birthright, regardless of the intervening Ancestors. My Claim is strengthened by the Fact that our Family has a Regular Coat-of-Arms. Everybody had forgotten about it for over Seven Hundred Years until Sister and I hired a Man to find it. Sister is now Lady Frost-Simpson and lives on the Other Side. When she discovered his Lordship he was down to his last Dickey. She took him out of Hock, and he is so Grateful that sometimes he lets me come and Visit them. I have seen the Prince."

"Then you are an Englishman?" queried the Traveler who had Bet that way.

"It is not admitted in London," was the sorrowful Reply. "Sometimes if Frost-Simpson has to come Home for Money while I am visiting Sister, he puts me up at the Clubs and all the Chaps seem to think I am an American. I try to be exactly like them, but I fail. They say I have an Accent, although I have been working all my Life to overcome it. I have not used the word 'Guess' for many Years."

"Yours is a Sad Case," remarked the Second Traveler. "Why do you ever come back?"

"To collect my Income," was the Reply. "Isn't it a Bore? Rents and all that sort of Rot, you know."

"But you have not settled the Bet," said one of the Persistent Travelers. "Are you a Yankee?"

"I have never Admitted it, and I cannot do so now," said the Brother-in-Law of Lord Frost-Simpson. "At the same time, it is on Record that I was born at Pontiac, Michigan. Of course, you know What I am Striving to be. But there must be a Handicap somewhere. During the Two Hundred Years in which my Ancestors temporarily resided in the States, they must have absorbed some

ANCESTOR

of the Characteristics of this Uncouth and Vulgar People, and as a Result the Sins of the Father are visited upon the Child even to the third and fourth Generations, and I cannot hold a Monocle in my Eye to save my Life. I live Abroad, and strive to Forget, and work hard to be just like the other Fellows, but I do not seem to Arrive. Even in this Beastly Country, where the Imitation Article usually passes current as the Real Thing, there seems to be some Doubt as to my Case, seeing that you two Persons have made this Bet. Concerning the Bet, I fear that I am unable to Decide it. I do not know What I am."

"I know What you are," said the First Traveler, "but I do not dare to tell you right here in the Car, because the Pullman Company has a Rule against the use of such Language."

So they declared the Bet off and went forward and sat in the Day Coach.

MORAL: *Be Something*.

THE FABLE OF THE ADULT GIRL WHO GOT BUSY BEFORE THEY COULD RING THE BELL ON HER

ONCE upon a Time there was a Lovely and Deserving Girl named Clara, who was getting so near Thirty that she didn't want to Talk about it. Everybody had a Good Word for her. She traveled with the Thoroughbreds, and was always Among Those Present; so it was hard to understand why she hadn't Married. Other Girls not as Good-Looking or Accomplished had been grabbed off while they were Buds. Already some of them were beginning to act as Chaperons for Clara. They were keeping Tab on Clara's Age, too, and began to think that she would land on the Bargain Counter, and have to be satisfied with a Widower who wore a Toupee and dyed his Eyebrows.

Clara was somewhat of a Mind-Reader. She knew that the Friends of her Youth were predicting a Hard Finish for her, so she decided to Fool them. And she knew that it Behooved her to Catch On before the Children started in to call her Auntie.

Now it is not to be inferred that Clara was what the Underwriters call a Bad Risk. She never had been a Drug on the Market. When she went to a Hop she did not have to wait for Ladies' Choice in order to swing into the Mazy. In fact, she had been Engaged now and then, just for Practice, and she had received Offers from some of the hold-over Bachelors who went around Proposing from Force of Habit. But Clara was not out for any man who had been Turned Down elsewhere. She wanted the Right Kind, and she was going to do the Picking herself.

Having made an Inventory of the Possibilities, she selected the Treasurer of the Shoe Factory, and decided that she could Love him without Straining herself. He was about her age, and was almost as good-looking as a Gibson Man, and had A1 Prospects. It would be no Easy Job to Land him, however, because the Competition was very keen and he was Wary, trying to be a Kind Friend to every Girl he knew, but playing no Favorites. He kept the Parents guessing. He had been Exposed to Matrimony so often without being Taken Down, that he was generally regarded as an Immune.

Clara got Busy with herself and hatched a Scheme. When all the Smart Set got ready to pike away for the Heated Term, Clara surprised her Friends by guessing that she would remain at Home. It was a Nervy Thing to do, because all the Social Head-Liners who could command the Price were supposed to flit off to a Summer Hotel, and loiter on the Pine Veranda and try to think they were Recuperating.

Clara told her Mother to go, as usual, but she would stay at Home and be a Companion to poor lonesome Papa. So all the Women went away to the Resorts with their Cameras and Talcum Powder and Witch Hazel, and Clara was left alone in Town with the Men.

It is a Traditional Fact that there is no Social Life in Town during the Dog Days. But there is nothing to prevent a Bright Girl from Starting Something. That is what Clara did.

She stocked up the Refrigerator, and hung a Hammock on the Lawn with a few Easy Chairs around it. The Young Men marooned in Town heard of the Good Thing, and no one had to tear their Garments to induce them to come. They arrived at the rate of from Seven to Twelve a Night, and dipped into Papa's Cigars and the Liquid Nourishment, regardless. Although Clara had remained in town to act as Companion to Papa, it was noticed that when she had all the Company in the Evening, Papa either had been Chloroformed and put to Bed or else he had his Orders to stay Under Cover.

Clara did not send for the Treasurer of the Shoe Factory. She knew better than to go out after her Prey. She allowed him to find his Way to the House with the others. When he came, she did not chide him for failing to make his Party Call; neither did she rush toward him with a Low Cry of Joy, thereby tipping her Hand. She knew that the Treasurer of the Shoe Factory was Next to all these Boarding School Tactics, and could not be Handled by the Methods that go with the College Students. Clara had enjoyed about ten years' Experience in handling the Creatures, and she had learned to Labor and to Wait. She simply led him into the Circle and took his Order, and allowed him to sit there in the

Gloaming and observe how Popular she was. All the men were Scrapping to see who would be Next to sit in the Hammock with her. It looked for a while as if Clara would have to give out Checks, the same as in a Barber Shop. Late that night when the Men walked homeward together, they remarked that Clara was a Miserable Hostess, they didn't think.

CLARA

Next Evening the Treasurer of the Shoe Factory was back on the Lawn. So were all the Others. They said there was no beating a Place where you could play Shirt-Waist Man under the Trees, and have a Fairy Queen in White come and push Cold Drinks at you and not have to sign any Ticket. They composed flattering Songs about Clara, and every time she moved there was a Man right there with a Sofa Cushion to help her to be Comfortable.

In the mean time, the Other Girls out at the Summer Resorts were doing the best they could with these High School Cadets, wearing Tidies around their Hats, who would rather go out in a Cat-Boat and get their arms tanned than remain on Shore and win the Honest Love of an American Girl, with a String to it.

Clara's work about this time was ever so Glossy. She began by asking the Treasurer of the Shoe Factory to come with her to the Refrigerator to get out some more Imported Ginger Ale. All the men Volunteered to help, and two or three wanted to Tag along, but Clara drove them back.

They were gone a Long Time, because the Treasurer had to draw all the Corks, and they Fussed around together in the Pantry fixing up a Lunch for the Boys. Clara told him how Strong and Handy he was, until he felt an increase in his Chest Measurement.

On successive evenings she had the Treasurer supervise all the Arrangements. The Hired Girl had every Evening off, because it was so much more Jolly to go out and run the place yourself. In less than a Week the Treasurer was giving Orders around the House. She would get him back to the Kitchen and tie an Apron around him and ask what she should do next. She made him out to be the Only One who could be Trusted. The others were Company, but he was like one of the Family. And although he was being Worked like Creamy Butter, he never Suspected.

Her Game was to Domesticate him in Advance, and let him have a Foretaste of what it is to be Boss of your own House, except as to the Bills. The Pantry was full of Home Delicacies such as he couldn't get at the Hotel, and the Service was the best ever. Clara was right at his Elbow with a Willing Smile.

It didn't take him long to realize that he was missing a lot by remaining Single. He wondered why he had been so slow in getting

on to Clara's Good Points. Also he wondered if it was any
Open-and-Shut Certainty when a dozen other Men, some of them
Younger and more Gallus, were after her in Full Cry.

Clara had him Pulled In, Strung and Hung over the side of
the Boat.

Of course if all the other Girls had been in Town, they would
have Tumbled long before it ran into a Certainty, and probably
they would have formed a V and rushed in to break up the Play.

HIGH-SCHOOL CADET

But the other Girls were Far Away with the Old Men and the Seminary Striplings. Clara had an Open Field, with no need of any Interfering or Blocking, and if she Fell Down it was her own Fault. Besides, she had all these other Admirers set out as Decoys to prove that if he didn't, somebody else might.

The Treasurer of the Shoe Factory got a large Rally on himself, and she had to Give In and make a Promise.

He loves to tell Callers how he proposed to his Wife in the Kitchen, and he doesn't know to this Day that she was Expecting it.

MORAL: *As soon as he begins to Frequent the Back Rooms of the House, measure him for the Harness.*

THE FABLE OF THE INVETERATE JOKER WHO REMAINED IN MONTANA

THE Subject of this Fable started out in Life as a Town Cut-Up. He had a keen Appreciation of Fun, and was always playing Jokes. If he wanted a few Gum-Drops he would go into the Candy Store and get them, and then ask the Man if he was willing to take Stamps. If the Man said he was, then the Boy would stamp a couple of times, which meant that the Laugh was on the Man. It was considered a Great Sell in Those Parts.

Or else he would go into a Grocery with another tricky Tad and get some Article of Value, and they would pretend to Quarrel as to which should Pay for it. One would ask the Proprietor if he cared who paid for it, and if he said he did not, they would up and tell him to Pay for it Himself. This one was so Cute that they had a little Piece in the Paper about it.

Or they would go and Purchase a Watermelon to be paid for as soon as a Bet was decided, and afterwards it would Develop that the Bet was whether the Saw-Mill would fall to the East or the West, in case the Wind blew it over.

It was Common Talk that the Boy was Sharp as a Tack and Keen as a Brier and a Natural-Born Humorist.

Once he sold a Calf to the Butcher, several Hours after the Calf had been struck by Lightning. As for ordering Goods and having them charged to his Father, that was one of the Slickest Things he ever did.

About the time the Joker was old enough to leave Home, he traveled out through the Country selling Bulgarian Oats to the Farmers. When the Contract for the Seed Oats got around to the Bank, it proved to be an iron-clad and double-riveted Promissory Note. The Farmer always tried to get out of Paying it, but when the Case came to Trial and the Jurors heard how the Agent palavered the Hay-Seed they had to Snicker right out in Court. They always gave Judgment for the Practical Joker, who would take them out and buy Cigars for them, and they would hit him on the Back and tell him he was a Case.

One Day the Joker had an Inspiration, and he had to tell it to a Friend, who also was something of a Wag.

They bought a Cat-Tail Swamp remote from Civilization and divided it into Building Lots. The Marsh was Advertised as a Manufacturing Suburb, and they had side-splitting Circulars showing the Opera House, the Drill Factory, Public Library, and the Congregational Church. Lots were sold on the Instalment Plan to Widows, Cash-Boys, and Shirt-Factory Girls who wanted to get Rich in from fifteen to twenty Minutes.

The Joker had a Lump of Bills in every Pocket. If asked how he made his Roll, he would start to Tell, and then he would Choke Up, he was so full of Laugh. He certainly had a Sunny Disposition.

Finally he went to the State of Montana. He believed he could have a Season of Merriment by depositing some Valuable Ore in a Deserted Mine, and then selling the Mine to Eastern Speculators. While he was Salting the Mine, pausing once in a while to Control his Mirth, a few Natives came along, and were Interested. They were a slow and uncouth Lot, with an atrophied Sense of Humor, and the Prank did not Appeal to them. They asked the Joker to Explain, and before he could make it Clear to them or consult his Attorney they had him Suspended from a Derrick. He did not Hang straight enought to suit, so they brought a Keg of Nails and tied to his Feet, and then stood off and Shot at the Buttons on the Back of his Coat.

MORAL: *Don't Carry a Joke too far, and never Carry it into Montana.*

MANUFACTURING SUBURB

THE FABLE OF THE CRUEL INSULT AND THE ARRIVAL OF THE LOVER FROM NO. 6

ONE Morning there came into the Dining Room of the Peerless Hotel at Welby's Junction an English Tourist and the Advance Agent of the Mabel Mooney Repertoire Company.

They took their Places at the Table underneath a Chromo representing a Pyramid of Idealized Fruit. The Table was covered with Sail Cloth, and in the Center was the Corroded Caster, which gave out a Sound similar to that of the Galloping Horse in the War Drama whenever any one walked across the Floor.

The English Traveler appeared to have received Bad News from Home, but he had not. That was the Normal Expression. His Mustache was long and wilted. Also the Weary Look around the Eyes. He traveled with a Cowhide Bag that must have used up at least one Cow. The Clothes he wore evidently had been cut from a Steamer Rug by his Mother, or some other Aged Relative suffering from Astigmatism. He had been Sleeping in them.

As for the Second Traveler, he was an Advance Agent.

"Cheer Up," said the Advance Agent to the English Tourist. "It may not be True, and if it is True it may be for the Best."

The English Tourist made no Response, fearing that his Fellow-Traveler might be In Trade.

Then the One that waited on the Table did the Glide from behind a Screen.

She was very Pale, up to a certain Point.

Pausing about six feet from the English Tourist she looked resolutely at a Knot-Hole in the Floor and said:

"Beefsteakliverhamand."

"My Good Woman," said the Man from Stoke-on-Tritham, just as if he meant to Prorogue something. "I should like a Rasher of Bacon, and have it Jolly Well Done."

"Ain't got no Bacon," she replied, feeling of her Brooch.

"Dyuh me! Then I should like some Boiled Eggs, and mind that they are Fresh."

"I'll give you Regular Aigs," she said, lifting her Head proudly, for she was no Serf.

"Approach me, Kit," said the Advance Agent, with gentle Voice.

"Is tha-a-at so-o-o?" she asked. "I'll have you know, Smarty, my name ain't Kit. So There!"

"Well, make it Genevieve," said the Advance Agent. "Come

TOURIST

close and hold my Hand while I give you this Order. And merely as one Friend speaking to another, I want to tell you that the Blending under the Left Ear is very poor, and if you are not careful somebody will Sign you as a Spotted Girl."

"My Mother was a Lady," she said.

"That being the Case, I would like to have you go out and Engage a nice piece of Liver for me. And if you show yourself to be real Winsome and Chic I may be able to use you with the Troupe."

"Tea or Coffee?"

"Don't tell me which one you bring and see if I can Guess. And I would like some Actual Potatoes."

"I suppose, Sir, you think I have no Feelings."

"That is none of my Business," he replied. "I am merely passing through your Beautiful Little City."

"I wish Edmund was here," said she.

"So do I," assented the Advance Agent, promptly. "If he can wait on the Table I wish he was here. Now see if you can make the Kitchen in two Jumps."

"He'd show you if you could get Flossy with a Lady, even though she Works."

"You are about to lose your Tip, standing around here trying to shoot it back at the Handsome Guest," remarked the Advance Agent. "Has Edmund about finished his Fall Plowing?"

"He don't do no Fall Plowing," was the Bitter Reply. "He Fires on Number Six."

At that Moment there entered a Railroad Boy with Braid on his Clothes and Coal-Dust on his Neck. He removed the Cap that had rested on his flanging Ears and sat at the Table with the Advance Agent and the English Tourist.

"Feed me Everything, with One in the Light to come along," he said. "If any of the Cockroaches ask for me, tell them I'm for all Night with the Yellow Rattlers, and laid out at Winona."

The English Tourist was holding his Head.

"I guess you won't carry on so Gay since he's come," said the Sensitive Waitress, addressing the Advance Agent.

"Did he Call you Down?" asked Edmund, the Loving Fireman, glancing at the Advance Agent.

"He used me like I was the Dirt under his Feet," she replied, placing her Hand on her Breast and biting her Lower Lip.

"Well, it's a Good Thing," said Edmund. "You've needed a few of them Jolts ever since you had your Hand read by the Gypsy and started to read that Bertha Clay Book. It's a good thing to have a Strong Josher come along now and then, just to

ADVANCE AGENT

show you Proud Dolls how to take a Joke. Do I Eat?"

The Sensitive Waitress hurried Away, feeling hurt.

"Overlook all the Phoney Acting by the Little Lady, Bud," said the Fireman to the Advance Agent. "She's only twenty-seven."

Producing a small Note-Book, the English Traveler said: "Gentlemen, I regard this Incident as Most Extraordinary and somewhat Mystifying. I fear that I am not sufficiently acquainted with your Vernacular to grasp the full Purport of what has occurred here. Will you Explain it to me?"

"Did you notice the Ingenue that guaranteed you the Regular Eggs," asked the Advance Agent.

"You mean the Young Woman who was here a moment ago?"

"That's the Party! You saw her?"

"Certainly."

"Now, I'll tell you all about it, if you promise not to put it in your Book."

"Really, you know, I had intended to Use it," said the Traveler.

"All right, then; put it in, but don't use any Names. This is Under the Rose, remember. The Proud Working Girl that was in here just now is my Sister."

And the Englishman was deeply Perplexed.

MORAL: *Brothers in Name only.*

WORKING GIRL

THE FABLE *OF THE* LODGE FIEND, *AND THE* DELILAH TRICK PLAYED *BY* HIS WIFE

A WOMAN who had done nothing to Deserve it was the Wife of a Joiner. He was the K. G. of one Benevolent Order and the Worshipful High Guy of something else, and the Senior Warden of the Sons of Patoosh, and a lot more that she couldn't keep track of.

When he got on all of his Pins he had Sousa put away.

Night after Night he was off to a Hall up a Dark Stairway to land some Unfortunate into the Blue Lodge or the Commandery or else Over the Hot Sands.

He carried at least twenty Rituals in his Head, and his Hands were all twisted out of Shape from giving so many different Grips.

In the Morning when he came out of the House he usually found some one waiting on the Door-Step to give him the Sign of Distress and work the fraternal Pan-Handle on him. He subscribed for the Magazines that were full of these sparkling Chapter Reports, and after that, if he had not spent all his money going to Conclaves and Grand Lodge Meetings, he paid Dues and Assessments and bought Uniforms. He had one Suit in particular, with Frogs and Cords and Gold Braid strung around over the Front of it, and then a Helmet with about a Bushel of Red Feathers. When he got into this Rig and strapped on his Jeweled Sword he wouldn't have traded Places with Nelson A. Miles.

His Wife often said that he ought not to leave her and take up with a Goat, and that she could use on Groceries some of the Coin that he was devoting to Velvet Regalia and Emblematic Watch-Charms, but he always tried to make it Right with her by explaining that he had Insurance in most of these Whispering Organizations, so that she and the Children would come in for a whole Wad of Money. The Wife thought it was too long to wait. He seemed to be in a Fair Way to live another Century and keep on paying Assessments.

There was no use in Arguing with him. When a Man gets to be

a confirmed Joiner he is not Happy unless he can get into an unlighted Room two or three Nights a Week, and wallop the Neophyte with a Stuffed Club, and walk him into a Tub of Water, and otherwise Impress him with the Solemnity of the Ordeal.

THE JOINER

The real Joiner loves to sit up on an elevated Throne, wearing a Bib and holding a dinky Gavel, and administer a blistering Oath to the Wanderer who seeks the Privilege of helping to pay the Rent.

To a Man who does not cut very many Lemons around his own House, where they are Onto him, it is a great Satisfaction to get up in a Lodge Hall and put on a lot of Ceremonial Dog, and have the Members kneel in front of him and Salute him as the Exalted Sir Knight.

You take a Man who is Plugging along on a Salary, and who has to answer the 'Phone and wrap up Tea all Day, and let him go out at Night and be an Exalted Sir, and it helps him to feel that he isn't such a Nine-Spot after all.

Now this particular Joiner wanted to be up on a carpeted Dais every blessed Evening, having the Brothers march in front of him and give him the High Office. His Wife, being unacquainted with the Secrets of the Lodge Room, was unable to understand why he was so Fascinated with the Life. She was exceedingly Inquisitive and often tried to Pump him by the most Artful Methods, but of course he did not dare to Divulge or his Right Arm would have Withered and his Tongue would have Cleaved to the Roof of his Mouth, and he would have been an Outcast on the Face of the Earth, despised by all other Members of the Royal Tararum. Now and then he Talked in his Sleep, and she caught Expressions in regard to Branding him on the Other Leg or putting him back into the Coffin, and her Curiosity was intensified.

One day she read in a Veracious Newspaper that if the Left Hand of a Sleeping Person be immersed in Tepid Water, then the Sleeper will truthfully answer any Question that may be asked. She resolved to try it on her Husband. She was dying to know what they Said and Did at Lodge Meetings that would keep a Man away from Home so many Nights in the Week.

That Night after he had come home from the Odd Fellows and passed into Slumber she crept out and took a Low Advantage of him. She slid his Left Hand into a bowl of Warm Water without arousing him, and he Gave Up. He told all the Passwords, the Secret Mottoes, the Oaths, the Meaning of the Symbols and the Unwritten Work. When he had finished she had a Notion to Ring for a Night Cab and go Home to her own Family, but her Better Judgment prevailed. She concluded that she would have to continue to Live with him, no matter what she Thought of him.

She never dared to tell that she Knew, and he never Suspected. Husband never guessed why it was that when he started out for an Evening with the Skeletons and the Candidates she stood back and smiled at him more in Pity than in Anger.

MORAL: *It's a Good Thing they don't Know.*

THE FABLE OF THE APPREHENSIVE
SPARROW AND HER DAILY ESCAPE

ONCE there was a Proper little Female who Fluttered and
was interested in Movements. She was born the Year that
Fremont ran against Buchanan. All she knew about Spooning
was that she had Read in Ella Wheeler Wilcox. Time and again
she said that if a Man ever attempted to Take Liberties with her,
she knew she would Die of Mortification. At Last Reports she
was Living, but she had Courted Death at least Fifteen Hundred
Times.

If a Strange Man came up behind her while she was walking
Homeward in the Dusk, she always gave a Timid Glance behind
and Hurried, suspecting that he would Overtake her and seize
her by both Wrists and tell her not to Scream. She would reach
her own Door and lean against it, almost in a Swoon, and the
Strange Man would pass by, softly Humming to Himself.

Occasionally an Adventurer with Coal-Black Eyes and a
Suspicious Manner would come and sit right beside her in a Car,
evidently for some Purpose, and she would close her Lips tightly
and resolve to do a Steve Brodie out of the Window if she saw
his Hand slipping over toward Hers. Fortunately, the man kept
his Eyes on the Sporting Page and made no Move.

If she happened to be in the Waiting-Room at the Station,
and a coarse but masterful Claim Agent, or some one else equally
Terrifying, happened to come across the Room at her, she could
feel her Little Heart stand still, and she would say, "This is where
I get it." After he had gone past, on his way to the Check-Room,
she would put some Camphor on her Handkerchief and declare
to Goodness that never again would she start out to Travel unless
she had some Older Person with her.

More than once when she was at Home, with only a few other
Persons around the House, she saw a Large Man come up the
Front Steps, and she would be Frozen with Terror, and could
see herself being lifted into a Closed Carriage by the Brutal
Confederates. She would slip a Pair of Scissors under her Apron

and creep to the Front Door, prepared to Resist with all her Girlish Strength, and the Man would have to talk to her through the Door, and ask where they wanted the Coal delivered.

Now and then a Caller would find her Reviving herself with a Cup of Tea.

The Caller would say: "Madge, Child, you are as Pale as a Ghost."

THE SPARROW

Madge would reply: "Oh, I have just had such a Turn! I was out watering the Nasturtiums, when a Man in a Crash Suit came along the Street and looked right at me. The Gate was open, and there was nothing to prevent him from coming right in and Getting me."

The Appalled Visitor would want to know what became of him, and Madge would explain that he turned at the Next Corner, and she had been as Weak as a Cat ever since.

On her Shopping Expeditions she noticed Dozens of Men, apparently Trailing right along after her, and she knew that her only Salvation was to look straight ahead and indicate by her Bearing that she was no Flirt. By so doing she eluded many a one who wanted to Catch Step with her and begin a Conversation.

The Collected Stories of her Successful but Hair-Breadth Escapes from Men of the World, who semed to Forget that all Women were not Alike, would have filled a Volume bigger than the Family Medicine Book.

Happily, no one ever went Quite So Far. She invariably Escaped.

MORAL: *Don't Worry*.

THE FABLE *OF THE* REGULAR CUSTOMER *AND THE* COPPER-LINED ENTERTAINER

O NE day the Main Works of a Wholesale House was Jacking Up the Private Secretary and getting ready to close his desk for the Day, when in blew a Country Customer. The Head of the Concern would have given Seven Dollars if he could have got out and caught the Elevated before the Country Customer showed up. However, he was Politic, and he knew he must not throw down a Buyer who discounted his Bills and was good as Old Wheat. So he gave a Correct Imitation of a Man who is tickled nearly to Death. After calling the Country Customer "Jim," he made him sit down and tell him about the Family, and the Crops, and Collections, and the Prospects for Duck-Shooting. Then, selecting an opportune moment, he threw up Both Hands. He said he had almost forgotten the Vestry Meeting at Five O'clock, and going out to Dinner at Six-Thirty. He was about to Call Off the Vestry Meeting, the Dinner, and all other Engagements for a Week to come, but Jim would not Listen to it. As a Compromise the Head of the Concern said he would ask their Mr. Byrd to take charge of the Country Customer. They could surely find some Way of putting in the Evening. He said the Oratorio Club was gong to sing at Music Hall, and also there was a Stereopticon Lecture on India. Jim said he would prefer the Stereopticon Show, because he loved to look at Pictures.

The Head of the Concern said that the Country Customer would be sure to like their Mr. Byrd. Everybody liked Byrd. His Full Name was Mr. Knight Byrd.

He pushed on a few Buttons and blew into several snaky Tubes and put the whole Shop on the Jump to find Mr. Byrd. The latter happened to be in a Rathskeller not far away. When he heard that there was Work to be done in his Department he brushed away the Crumbs and Hot-Footed up to see the Boss.

In presenting Mr. Byrd to the Country Customer the Head of the Concern laid it on with a Shovel. He said that Jim Here was his Friend, and the House considered it an Honor to Entertain him. The Country Customer sat there feeling Sheepish and Unworthy but a good deal Puffed Up just the same. Then the Head of the Firm made his Escape and the Country Customer was in the Hands of Mr. Byrd.

Mr. Byrd was known in the Establishment as the Human Expense Account. No one had ever accused him of being a Quitter. He was supposed to be Hollow inside. Whenever any Friend of the Firm showed up, Mr. Byrd was called upon to take charge of him and Entertain him to a Stand-Still. The Boss was troubled with Dyspepsia, and Conscientious Scruples, and a Growing Family, and a few other Items that prevented him from going out at Night with the Visiting Trade. He had it arranged to give each one of them a choice Mess of Beautiful Language and then pass him along to Mr. Byrd.

Mr. Byrd was a Rosy and Red-Headed Gentleman with a slight Overhang below the Shirt Front. He breathed like a Rusty Valve every time he had to go up a Stairway, but he had plenty of Endurance of another Kind. For Years he had been playing his Thirst against his Capacity, and it was still a Safe Bet, whichever Way you wanted to place your Money. His Batting Average was about Seven Nights to the Week. He discovered that Alcohol was a Food long before the Medical Journals got onto it.

Mr. Byrd's chief value to the Wholesale House lay in the Fact that he could Meet all Comers and close up half the Places in Town, and then show up next Morning with a Clean Collar and a White Carnation, and send in word to lead out another Country Customer.

Mr. Byrd's first Move was to take Jim to a Retreat that was full of Statuary and Paintings. It was owned by a gray-haired Beau named Bob, who was a Ringer for a United States Senator, all except the White Coat. Bob wanted to show them a new Tall One called the Mamie Taylor, and after they had Sampled a Couple Jim said it was all right and he believed he would take one. Then he told Bob how much he had taken in the Year before and what his Fixtures cost him, and if anybody didn't think he was Good they could look him up in Bradstreet or Dun, that was all. He said he was a Gentleman, and that no Cheap Skate in a Plug Hat could tell him where to Get Off. This last Remark was intended for an inoffensive Person who had slipped in to get a Rhine Wine and Seltzer, and was pronging about Forty Cents' Worth of Lunch.

They got around Jim and Quieted him, and Mr. Byrd suggested

"HOORAY! HOORAY!"

that they go and Eat something before they got too Busy. The
Country Customer would not leave the Art Buffet until Bob had
promised to come down and Visit him sometime. When they got
into the Street again the Country Customer noticed that all the
Office Buildings were set on the Bias, and they were introducing
a new style of spiral Lamp-Post.

They dined at a Palm-Garden that had Padding under the
Table-Cloth and a Hungarian Orchestra in the Corner. Mr.
Byrd ordered Eleven Courses, and then asked Jim what Kind he
usually had with his Dinner. This is an Awful Question to pop
at a Man who has been on Rain Water and Buttermilk all his Life.
Jim was not to be Fazed. He said that he never ordered any
Particular Label for fear People might think he was an Agent.
That was the Best Thing that Jim said all Evening.

Mr. Byrd told the Waiter to stand behind Jim and keep Busy.
When Jim began to Make Signs that he could not Stand any more,
the Entertainer told him to Inhale it and rub it in his Hair.

Along toward Dessert Jim was talking in the Tone used by
Muggsy McGraw when he is Coaching the Man who is Playing
Off from Second. He was telling how much he Loved his Wife.
She would have been Pleased to hear it.

Mr. Byrd paid a Check that represented One Month's Board
down where Jim lived. They fell into a Horseless Hansom and
went to see the Hity-Tity Variety and Burlesque Aggregation in a
new Piece entitled "Hooray! Hooray!" Jim sat in a Box for the
First Time, and wanted to throw Money on the Stage. The Head
Usher had to come around once in a while to ask him not to let
his Feet hang over, and to remember that the Company could do
all the Singing without any Help from him. Mr. Byrd sat back
slightly Flushed and watched the Country Customer make a Show
of himself. It was an Old Story to him. He knew that the quiet
School Trustee kind of a Man who goes Home at Sundown for
364 Days in the Year, with the Morning Steak and a Roll of
Reading Matter under his Arm, is the worst Indian in the World
when he does find himself among the Tall Houses and gets it Up
his Nose.

He allowed Jim to stand and Yell when the Chorus struck the
Grand Finale, and a little later on, when they had chartered a

low-necked Carriage and Jim wanted to get up and Drive, he Stood for it, although he had to make a Pretty Talk to a couple of Policemen before he landed Jim at the Hotel.

If this were a Novel, there would be a Row of Stars inserted right here.

JIM

The Sun was high in the Heavens when the Country Customer opened his Eyes and tried to Remember and then tried to Forget. Some one was sitting at his Bedside. It was Mr. Byrd, the Long-Distance Entertainer, looking as Sweet and Cool as a Daisy.

"Before I give you the Photograph of Myself which you requested last Night, would you care for anything in the way of Ice Water?" he asked.

Jim did a sincere Groan, and said he could use a Barrel of it.

"Did I request a Photograph?" he asked, as he felt for the Boundaries of his Head.

"You did," replied the Entertainer. "And you gave me your Watch as a Keepsake. I have brought the Watch and all the Money you had left after you bought the Dog."

"What Dog?"

"The Dog that you gave to Bob."

"Did we go back there again? I remember the First Time."

"Yes, it was In There that you wanted to Run a Hundred Yards with any Man Present for Chalk, Money, or Marbles."

"Where are we now—at the Hotel?"

"Yes, and Everything is Smoothed Over. The Night Clerk has agreed not to swear out a Warrant."

Jim did not Comprehend, but he was afraid to Ask.

"It may be that I was a mite Polluted," he suggested.

"You were a teeny bit Pickled about Two, when you tried to upset the Lunch Wagon, but I don't think any one Noticed it," said Mr. Byrd.

"Take me to the Noon Train," requested the Country Customer. "Tell the Conductor where I live, and send me the Bills for all that I have Broken."

"Everything is Settled," responded the Entertainer. "But why Tear yourself away?"

"I am Through," replied Jim, "So why Tarry?"

Mr. Byrd took him to the Train and arranged with the Porter of the Parlor Car for a Pillow.

When the Country Customer arrived at Home he accounted for the Eyes by saying that the Night Traffic makes so much Noise on these Hard Stone Pavements, it is almost impossible to get the usual amount of Sleep.

The Head of the Concern put his O. K. on a Voucher for $43.60, and it occurred to him that Stereopticon Lectures seemed to be Advancing, but he asked no Questions.

Ever after that Jim bought all his Goods of this one House. He had to.

MORAL: *Scatter Seeds of Kindness.*

THE FABLE OF LUTIE, THE FALSE ALARM, AND HOW SHE FINISHED ABOUT THE TIME THAT SHE STARTED

LUTIE was an Only Child. When Lutie was eighteen her Mother said they ought to do something with Lutie's Voice. The Neighbors thought so, too. Some recommended killing the Nerve, while others allowed that it ought to be Pulled.

But what Mamma meant was that Lutie ought to have it Cultivated by a Professor. She suspected that Lutie had a Career awaiting her, and would travel with an Elocutionist some day and have her Picture on the Programme.

Lutie's Father did not warm up to the Suggestion. He was rather Near when it came to frivoling away the National Bank Lithographs. But pshaw! The Astute Reader knows what happens in a Family when Mother and the Only Child put their Heads together to whipsaw the Producer. One Day they shouldered him into a Corner and extorted a Promise. Next Day Lutie started to Take.

She bought a red leather Cylinder marked "Music," so that people would not take it to be Lunch. Every Morning about 9 o'clock whe would wave the Housework to one side and tear for a Trolley.

Her Lessons cost the Family about twenty cents a Minute. She took them in a large Building full of Vocal Studios. People who didn't know used to stop in front of the Place and listen, and think it was a Surgical Institute.

There were enough Soprani in this one Plant to keep Maurice Grau stocked up for a Hundred Years. Every one thought she was the Particular One who would sooner or later send Melba back to Australia and drive Sembrich into the Continuous. Lutie was just about as Nifty as the Next One.

When she was at Home she would suck Lemons and complain about Draughts and tell why she didn't like the Other Girls' Voices. She began to act like a Prima Donna, and her Mother was encouraged a Lot. Lutie certainly had the Artistic Temperament bigger than a Church Debt.

Now before Lutie started in to do Things to her Voice she occasionally Held Hands with a Young Man in the Insurance Business, named Oliver. This Young Man thought that Lutie was all the Merchandise, and she regarded him as Permanent Car-Fare.

But when Lutie began to hang out at the Studios she took up with the Musical Set that couldn't talk about anything but

LUTIE

Technique and Shading and the Motif and the Vibrato. She began to fill up the Parlor with her new Friends, and the first thing Oliver knew he was in the Side Pocket and out of the Game.

In his own Line this Oliver was as neat and easy-running as a Red Buggy, but when you started him on the topic of Music he was about as light and speedy as a Steam Roller. Ordinarily he knew how to behave himself in a Flat, and with a good Feeder to work back at him he could talk about Shows and Foot-Ball Games and Things to Eat, but when any one tried to draw him out on the Classics, he was unable to Qualify.

When Lutie and her Musical acquaintances told about Shopan and Batoven he would sit back so quiet that often he got numb below the Hips. He was afraid to move his Feet for fear some one would notice that he was still in the Parlor and ask him how he liked Fugue No. 11, by Bock. He had never heard of any of these People, because they did not carry Tontine Policies with his Company.

Oliver saw that he would have to Scratch the Musical Set or else begin to Read Up, so he changed his Route. He canceled all Time with Lutie, and made other Bookings.

Lutie then selected for her Steady a Young Man with Hair who played the 'Cello. He was so wrapped up in his Art that he acted Dopey most of the time, and often forgot to send out the Laundry so as to get it back the same Week. Furthermore, he didn't get to the Suds any too often. He never Saw more than $3 at one time; but when he snuggled up alongside of a 'Cello and began to tease the long, sad Notes out of it, you could tell that he had a Soul for Music. Lutie thought he was Great, but what Lutie's Father thought of him could never get past the Censor. Lutie's Father regarded the whole Musical Set as a Fuzzy Bunch. He began to think that in making any Outlay for Lutie's Vocal Training he had bought a Gold Brick. When he first consented to her taking Lessons his Belief was that after she had practiced for about one Term she would be able to sit up to the Instrument along in the Dusk before the Lamps were lit, and sing "When the Corn is Waving, Annie Dear," "One Sweetly Solemn Thought," or else "Juanita." These were the Songs linked in his Memory with some Purple Evenings of the Happy Long Ago. He knew they were

Chestnuts, and had been called in, but they suited him, and he thought that inasmuch as he had put up the Wherewith for Lutie's Lessons he ought to have some kind of a Small Run for his Money.

Would Lutie sing such Trash? Not she. She was looking for Difficult Arias from the Italian, and she found many a one that was Difficult to sing, and probably a little more Difficult to Listen To.

CRITIC

The Voice began to be erratic, also. When father wanted to sit by the Student's Lamp and read his Scribner's, she would decide to hammer the Piano and do the whole Repertoire.

But when Mother had Callers and wanted Lutie to Show Off, then she would hang back and have to be Coaxed. If she didn't have a Sore Throat, then the Piano was out of Tune, or else she had left all of her Good Music at the Studio, or maybe she just couldn't Sing without some one to Accompany her. But after they had Pleaded hard enough, and everybody was Embarrassed and sorry they had come, she would approach the Piano timidly and sort of Trifle with it for a while, and say they would have to make Allowances, and then she would Cut Loose and worry the whole Block. The Company would sit there, every one showing the Parlor Face and pretending to be entranced, and after she got through they would Come To and tell her how Good she was.

She made so many of these Parlor Triumphs that there was no Holding her. She had herself Billed as a Nightingale. Often she went to Soirees and Club Entertainments, volunteering her Services, and nowhere did she meet a Well-Wisher who took her aside and told her she was a Shine—in fact, the Champion Pest.

No, Lutie never got out of her Dream until she made a bold Sashay with a Concert Company. It was her Professional Debut.

Father fixed it. The Idea of any one paying Real Money to hear Lutie sing struck him as being almost Good enough to Print. But she wouldn't be Happy until she got it, and so she Got It right where the Newport Lady wears the Rope of Pearls.

On the First Night the mean old Critics, who didn't know her Father or Mother, and had never been entertained at the House, came and got in the Front Row, and defied Lutie to come on and Make Good. Next Morning they said that Lutie had Blow-Holes in her Voice; that she hit the Key only once during the Evening, and then fell off backward; that she was a Ham, and her Dress didn't fit her, and she lacked Stage Presence. They expressed Surprise that she should be attempting to Sing when any bright Girl could learn to pound a Type-Writer in Four Weeks. They wanted to know who was responsible for her Appearance, and said it was a Shame to String these Jay Amateurs. Lutie read the Criticisms, and went into Nervous Collapse. Her Mother was all Wrought Up, and said somebody ought to go and kill the Editors. Father bore up grimly.

Before Lutie was Convalescent he had the Difficult Italian Arias carted out of the house. The 'Cello Player came to call one Day, and he was given Minutes to get out of the Ward.

By the time Oliver looked in again Lutie was more than ready to pay some Attention to him. She is now doing a few quiet Vocalizations for her Friends. When some one who hasn't Heard tells her that she is good enough for Opera, they have to open the Windows and give her more Air.

MORAL: *When in Doubt, try it on the Box-Office.*

THE FABLE OF THE COTILLON LEADER FROM THE HUCKLEBERRY DISTRICT WITH THE INTERMITTENT MEMORY

A YOUNG Man who had made a Sudden Winning, and was beginning to act as Shawl-Holder and Emergency Errand-Boy for the Society Queens, seemed to have a great deal of Trouble with his Memory. If he met Any One who had started with him a few Years before, and who used to Stake him to a Meal-Ticket now and then, or let him have a Scarf-Pin when he had to go out and make a Front, he could not appear to remember the Man's Name or tell where he had seen him before. When he was in a Loge at the Play-House with Exclusive Ethel and her Friends, he might look down in the Parquette and see the Landlady who had carried him through a Hard Winter and accepted a Graceful Wave of the Hand when she really needed the Board Money, but he found it impossible to Place her. Even the People who came from his own Town, and who knew him when he was getting Five a Week and wearing Celluloid Cuffs, and who could relate the Family History if they wanted to Knock, they couldn't make him Remember, even when they stopped him on the Street and recalled such Humiliations as the Time he used to pick Cherries on the Shares, and how Odd he looked in his Brother's Made-Over Clothes.

This Young Man buried the Dead Past until his Memory was a Blank for the whole Period up to the Time that the President of the Fidelity National invited him to Dinner and he got his first Peek at a sure-enough Butler.

He had been a Genuine Aristocrat for about Eighteen Months, when he made a Mis-step and landed with his Face in the Gravel. The Gigantic Enterprise which he had been Promoting got into the Public Prints as a Pipe Dream. There was no more Capital coming from the Angels. He was back at the Post, with nothing to Show for his Bold Dash except a Wardrobe and an Appetite for French Cooking. Society gave him the Frozen Face, and all those who had been speaking of him as a Young Napoleon agreed

that he was a Dub. The Banks were trying to Collect on a lot of
Slow Notes that he had floated in his Palmy Days, and they
had a Proud Chance to Collect. He went into the Bankruptcy
Court and Scheduled $73,000 of Liabilities, the Assets being a
Hat-Box and a Set of Theatrical Posters.

AFFECTIONATE MASSAGE

When he had to go out and Rustle for a Job he was a Busy Hand-Shaker once more. The Blow seemed to have landed right on the Bump of Memory, and put his Recollecting Department into full Operation again. He could spot an Old Pal clear across the Street. He was rushing up to Obscure Characters that he had not seen in Eight Years, and he called each one of them "Old Man." It was now their Turn to do the Forgetful Business. The Tablets of his Memory read as clear as Type-Writing. Upon meeting any Friend of his Boyhood he did the Shoulder-Slap, and rang in the Auld Lang Syne Gag. He was so Democratic he was ready to Borrow from the Humblest. The same Acquaintances who had tried to Stand In with him when Things were coming his Way, were cutting off Street-Corners and getting down behind their Newspapers to escape the Affectionate Massage, beginning at the Hand and extending to the Shoulder-Blade. It was No Use. He remembered them all, and no one got Past him.

MORAL: *Don't begin to Forget until you have it in Government Bonds.*

THE FABLE *OF THE* HE-GOSSIP *AND THE* MAN'S WIFE *AND THE* MAN

ONCE upon a time there was a He-Gossip named Cyrenius Bizzy. Mr. Bizzy was Middle-Aged and had a Set of dark Chinchillas. He carried a Gold-Headed Cane on Sunday. His Job on this Earth was to put on a pair of Pneumatic Sneakers every Morning and go out and Investigate Other People's Affairs.

He called himself a Reformer, and he did all his Sleuthing in the line of Duty.

If he heard of a Married Man going out Cab-Riding after Hours or playing Hearts for Ten Cents a Heart or putting a Strange Woman on the Car, he knew it was his Duty to edge around and slip the Information to some one who would carry it to the Wife. He was such a Good Man himself that he wanted all the other Men to wear long sable Belshazzars on the Sub-Maxillary and come to him for Moral Guidance. If they would not do it, the only Thing left for him to do was to Warn their Families now and then and get them into Hot Water, thus demonstrating that the Transgressor must expect Retribution to fall on him with quite a Crash.

Sometimes he would get behind a Board Fence to see the Wife of the Postmaster break off a Yellow Rose and pass it over the Gate to the Superintendent of the High School. Then he would Hustle out on his Beat and ask People if they had heard the Talk that was Going Around. Of course it Grieved him to be compelled to Peddle such Stories, but he had to do it in the Interests of Morality. If Folks did not have a Pious Protector to spot Worldly Sin and then get after it with a Sharp Stick, the Community would probably go to the Dogs in less than no time. When he had a Disagreeable Task to Perform, such as letting a Merchant know that his Business Partner had been seen slightly Sprung at a Picnic, he always wished to get through with it as quickly as possible, so usually he Ran. He did not want any one else to beat him there, because the Other Fellow might not get it Right.

Next Door to Cyrenius Bizzy there lived a Family that needed Regulating. Cyrenius Bizzy knew that he had been Called to do the Regulating. The Family had too much Fun to suit Cy. The Neighbor never came over to ask Mr. Bizzy how late they had better Sit Up, or what Young Men the Girls ought to invite to the House. Cyrenius would have been glad to fix up a Set of Rules, for he was a Bureau of Advice, open at all Hours. He could tell People just how much Money they ought to Save every Week, and how often they ought to Lick the Children, and so on. But the Family that lived Next Door made Loud Sport of Mr. Bizzy, and had no use for his Counsel. They played Authors right in the Front Room with the Curtains up, and they Danced the Two-Step so that he could be sure to see it from where he was hidden behind the Evergreen Tree, and they ran the Ice-Cream Freezer on Sunday Morning, and sang College Songs nearly every Evening.

It kept the He-Gossip on the Go most of the time to let the Neighborhood know all the Details of these Debauches. It did very little Good. The Family did not want to be Reformed. He even wrote Anonymous Letters telling them how Depraved they were. They were so Brazen and Hardened they paid no Attention except to give him the Rowdy Hee-Ho when they saw him pottering around the Shrubbery in his Front Yard, pretending to be at Work, but really doing the Pinkerton Act, and keeping one Ear spread for a nice, juicy Bit of Scandal.

Mr. Bizzy watched the Family at all Hours of the Day and Night for many Months. Although convinced that they were Children of Belial and pretty Hard Nuts in general, he still hoped to Rescue them. He wondered if he could not Appeal to the Man's Wife. She was a Daughter of Iniquity, all right, but maybe she might listen to an Entreaty if it came from one who was Pure, and who could point out to her in Fatherly Kindness that she was leading her Family on a Short Cut to the Weeping and Wailing and Gnashing of Teeth.

One Day Mr. Bizzy got a quiet Tip from another Moral Detective, that the Man had stayed out until 2 A. M., at a Banquet given to a Militia Company, so he knew it was Time for him to Act. He lay in Ambush until the Coast was Clear, and then he went across the Dead-Line and caught her on the Piazza. She was Surprised to see him.

He told her all the Reports he had heard about her Husband, and said he was Sorry for her. He wondered if they couldn't get together a few of the Respectable Men and Women of the Neighborhood, and have a Talk with the Husband, and try to Pluck him as a Brand from the Burning. She listened with that

THE SCANDAL

Ominous Calm which always precedes the Iowa Cyclone that takes the Roof off the Court House and moves the Poor Farm into the Adjoining County. She said she would take her Husband aside and have a Confidential Chat with him, and if he wanted to be Plucked, then she would call in the Cyrenius Bizzy Association of Pluckers.

THE HE-GOSSIP

The He-Gossip went Home feeling that he was entitled to a Pedestal right in between Savonarola and Martin Luther.

When the Man came Home his Wife told him. He murmured something about the Last Straw and moved swiftly out of doors. Pulling up the Rover Stake from the Croquet Grounds as he ran, he cleared the Dividing Fence without touching his Hands and

A MAN

began to Clean House. In about a Second there was a Sound as if somebody had stubbed his Toe and dropped a Crockery Store. Then Cyrenius was seen to Break the Record for the Running Long Jump, off the Front Stoop into an Oleander Tub, while wearing a Screen Door. After him came the Worldly Husband. For several Minutes the Copse where once the Garden smiled was full of He-Gossip and Cries for Help.

When the Man came back to where his Wife stood with her Hand on her Heart, he reported that the He-Gossip would be found on top of the Grape-Arbor.

MORAL: *Any one hoping to do Something in the Rescue Line had better go further than Next Door.*

THE FABLE OF THE AUTHOR WHO WAS SORRY FOR WHAT HE DID TO WILLIE

AN Author was sitting at his Desk trying to pull himself together and grind out Any Old Thing that could be converted into Breakfast Food. It was his Off Day, however. His Brain felt as if some one had played a Mean Trick on him and substituted a Side-Order of Cauliflower. All he could do was to lean up against his Desk and make marks and Piffle his Time away. Between Scribbles he wrote a few Verses about, "When Willie Came to say Good Night." It was a Sad Effort. He made it almost as Salty as a Mother Song and filled it with Papa and Mamma and the Patter of Baby Feet. He used Love-Light and the Evening Prayer and the Heart-Strings and other venerable Paraphernalia. He had to commit Infanticide to make it Weepy enough for the last Stanza. The Author wrote this Stuff merely to Get Back at himself and see how Sloppy he could be. He did not intend to Print it, because he was not a Vendor of Death-Beds, and he shrank from making any violent Assault on the Sensibilities. So he tossed the Idle Product into the Waste-Basket and wondered if he was beginning to lose his Mind. With that Poem in his Right Hand he could have walked into Bloomingdale and no Questions Asked.

While he was still Backing Up and Jockeying for a Fair Start at his Day's Work, A Friend came in and sat on the Edge of the Desk, and told him to go right ahead and not pay any Attention.

Seeing the Crumpled Paper in the Basket, the Friend, who was Inquisitive, hooked it out and read the Lines. Presently, when the Author looked up, the Friend had big Tears rolling down his Cheeks and was Sniffling.

"This is the Best Thing you have ever done," said the Friend. "My God, but it is Pathetic! It will certainly Appeal to any one who has lost a Child."

"I have no desire to Manufacture any more Sorrow for the Bereaved," said the Author. "They have had Trouble enough. If I have to deal in White Caskets or tap the Lachrymal Glands in order to thrash out an Income, I will cease being an Author and go back to Work."

"But this Poem will touch any Heart," insisted the Friend. "As soon as I got into it I began to Cry. You can get a Good Price for this."

When it came down to a Business Basis, the Author Switched.

"Get what you can on it," he said. "It seems a Shame to go and Market that kind of Scroll-Work; still if it hits you, it may be Bad enough to affect others having the same Shape of Head. I need the Money and I have no Shame."

Thereupon the Friend sent the Verses to the Publisher of a Family Monthly that Percolates into every Postoffice in the Country. In a few Days there came a tear-stained Acceptance and a Check. The Author said it was just like Finding $22.50, and he thought that was the End of it.

But when the Verses came out in the Monthly he began to get Letters from all parts of the United States telling him how much Suffering and Opening of Old Wounds had been caused by his little Poem about Willie and how Proud he ought to be. Many who wrote expressed Sympathy for him, and begged him to Bear Up. These Letters dazed the Author. He never had owned any Boy named Willie. He did not so much as Know a Boy named Willie. He lived in an Office Building with a lot of Stenographers and Bill Clerks. If he had been the Father of a Boy named Willie, and Willie had ever come to tell him "Good Night" when he was busy at Something Else, probably he would have jumped at Willie and snapped a piece out of his Arm. Just the Same, the Correspondents wrote to him from All Over, and said they could read Grief in every Line of his Grand Composition.

That was only the Get-Away. The next thing he knew, some Composer in Philadelphia had set the Verses to Music and they were sung on the Stage with colored Lantern-Slide Pictures of little Willie telling Papa "Good Night" in a Blue Flat with Lace Curtains on the Windows and a Souvenir Cabinet of Chauncey Olcott on the What-Not. The Song was sold at Music Stores, and the Author was invited out to Private Houses to hear it Sung, but he was Light on his Feet and Kept Away.

Several Newspapers sent for his Picture, and he was asked to write a Sunday Article telling how and why he did it. He was asked to Contribute Verses of the same General Character to various Periodicals. Sometimes he would get away by himself and read the Thing over again, and shake his Head and Remark: "Well, if they are Right, then I must be Wrong, but to me it is Punk."

He had his Likeness printed in Advertisements which told the Public to read what the Author of "Willie's Good Night" had

LANTERN SLIDE

to say about their Lithia Water. Some one named a light, free-smoking Five-Cent Cigar after him, and he began to see Weird Paintings on the Dead Walls, and was Ashamed to walk along those Streets.

It came out that one of the Frohmans wanted to Dramatize the Masterpiece, and it was Rumored that Stuart Robson, Modjeska, Thomas Q. Seabrooke, Maude Adams, Dave Warfield, and Walker Whiteside had been requested to play the Part of Willie.

Every morning the Author would get up and say to himself that it could not go on much longer. He felt sure that the Public would come to its Senses some Day, and get after him with a Rope, but it didn't. His Fame continued to Spread and Increase. All those Persons who had not Read it claimed that they had, so as to be in Line, and he had the same old Floral Tributes handed to him Day after Day.

It was Terrible. He had gone to College and spent a large amount of Money irrigating and fertilizing his Mind, and he had Dreamed of writing Something that would be Strong enough for Charles Dudley Warner's Library of the World's Warmest Copy, in a Limited Edition of 20,000; but instead of landing with the Heavy-Weights he seemed Destined to achieve Greatness as the Author of a Boy's Size Poem, bearing about the same Relation to the Literature of the Ages that a May Howard Window Hanger does to Pure Art. He was Famous until he couldn't rest, but it was not the Brand he had Coveted.

He decided to Live It Down. He would Produce something Serious and Meritorious that would throw "Willie's Good Night" into the Shade. So he labored for Two Years on a Novel that analyzed Social Conditions, and every Reviewer said that here was a Volume by the Author of "Willie's Good Night." The Purchasers of the Book expected to take it Home and Read it and Weep. When they found that it did not contain any Dark Skies or Headstones, they felt that they had been Bilked out of $1.50 each. It was Suggested that the Author of "Willie's Good Night" was losing his Grip and seemed to have Written Himself Out.

He was not wholly Discouraged. He went out Lecturing on

the Occult, just to prove to People that he had been Misjudged. The Local Chairman always introduced him as the Celebrated Author of "Willie's Good Night." Frequently he was Dragged away to a Home to meet all the Big Guns of one of these Towns that call a Lecture a Show. After he had been on Exhibition for a Half Hour or so, the same as the Albino or the Man with the

LITTLE FERN

Elastic Skin in the Main Curio Hall, the Host would clear a Space
in the Center of the Room and announce that he was about to
spring a Delightful Surprise on their Distinguished Guest. Little
Fern, the Daughter of the County Recorder, was going to Speak
"Willie's Good Night."

There are Times and Times, but those were the Times when he
suffered Agony that went beyond the Limit.

The Author always knew the Verses were Bad enough to be
Wicked, but he never guessed how Yellow they really were until
he heard them recited by Little Girls who made the Full Stop at
the Comma instead of the Period. He used to lose a Pound a
Minute, and when he would start back to the Hotel his Shoes would
be Full of Cold Perspiration. Finally, when he began to decline
Invitations, against the advice of his Manager, it was said of
him that he was Eccentric and appeared to have a Case of the
Swell Head.

He had to retire into a Suburb, where he built a Wall around
his Premises and put up Signs against Trespassing. He had a
Chinaman for a Servant, because the Chinaman did not know he
was an Author, but supposed him to be a Retired Porch-Climber.

Thus he was enabled to Forget for an Hour or Two at a Time.

MORAL: *Refrain from Getting Gay with the Emotions.*

Catalog
of
DOVER BOOKS

BOOKS EXPLAINING SCIENCE

(Note: The books listed under this category are general introductions, surveys, reviews, and non-technical expositions of science for the interested layman or scientist who wishes to brush up. Dover also publishes the largest list of inexpensive reprints of books on intermediate and higher mathematics, mathematical physics, engineering, chemistry, astronomy, etc., for the professional mathematician or scientist. For our complete Science Catalog, write Dept. catrr., Dover Publications, Inc., 180 Varick Street, New York 14, N. Y.)

CONCERNING THE NATURE OF THINGS, Sir William Bragg. Royal Institute Christmas Lectures by Nobel Laureate. Excellent plain-language introduction to gases, molecules, crystal structure, etc. explains "building blocks" of universe, basic properties of matter, with simplest, clearest examples, demonstrations. 32pp. of photos; 57 figures. 244pp. 5⅜ x 8.
T31 Paperbound **$1.35**

MATTER AND LIGHT, THE NEW PHYSICS, Louis de Broglie. Non-technical explanations by a Nobel Laureate of electro-magnetic theory, relativity, wave mechanics, quantum physics, philosophies of science, etc. Simple, yet accurate introduction to work of Planck, Bohr, Einstein, other modern physicists. Only 2 of 12 chapters require mathematics. 300pp. 5⅜ x 8.
T35 Paperbound **$1.60**

THE COMMON SENSE OF THE EXACT SCIENCES, W. K. Clifford. For 70 years, Clifford's work has been acclaimed as one of the clearest, yet most precise introductions to mathematical symbolism, measurement, surface boundaries, position, space, motion, mass and force, etc. Prefaces by Bertrand Russell and Karl Pearson. Introduction by James Newman. 130 figures. 249pp. 5⅜ x 8.
T61 Paperbound **$1.60**

THE NATURE OF LIGHT AND COLOUR IN THE OPEN AIR, M. Minnaert. What causes mirages? haloes? "multiple" suns and moons? Professor Minnaert explains these and hundreds of other fascinating natural optical phenomena in simple terms, tells how to observe them, suggests hundreds of experiments. 200 illus; 42 photos. xvi + 362pp.
T196 Paperbound **$1.95**

SPINNING TOPS AND GYROSCOPIC MOTION, John Perry. Classic elementary text on dynamics of rotation treats gyroscopes, tops, how quasi-rigidity is induced in paper disks, smoke rings, chains, etc, by rapid motion, precession, earth's motion, etc. Contains many easy-to-perform experiments. Appendix on practical uses of gyroscopes. 62 figures. 128pp.
T416 Paperbound **$1.00**

A CONCISE HISTORY OF MATHEMATICS, D. Struik. This lucid, easily followed history of mathematics from the Ancient Near East to modern times requires no mathematical background itself, yet introduces both mathematicians and laymen to basic concepts and discoveries and the men who made them. Contains a collection of 31 portraits of eminent mathematicians. Bibliography. xix + 299pp. 5⅜ x 8. T255 Paperbound **$1.75**

THE RESTLESS UNIVERSE, Max Born. A remarkably clear, thorough exposition of gases, electrons, ions, waves and particles, electronic structure of the atom, nuclear physics, written for the layman by a Nobel Laureate. "Much more thorough and deep than most attempts . . . easy and delightful," CHEMICAL AND ENGINEERING NEWS. Includes 7 animated sequences showing motion of molecules, alpha particles, etc. 11 full-page plates of photographs. Total of nearly 600 illus. 315pp. 6⅛ x 9¼. T412 Paperbound **$2.00**

WHAT IS SCIENCE?, N. Campbell. The role of experiment, the function of mathematics, the nature of scientific laws, the limitations of science, and many other provocative topics are explored without technicalities by an eminent scientist. "Still an excellent introduction to scientific philosophy," H. Margenau in PHYSICS TODAY. 192pp. 5⅜ x 8.
S43 Paperbound **$1.25**

FADS AND FALLACIES IN THE NAME OF SCIENCE, Martin Gardner. The standard account of the various cults, quack systems and delusions which have recently masqueraded as science: hollow earth theory, Atlantis, dianetics, Reich's orgone theory, flying saucers, Bridey Murphy, psionics, irridiagnosis, many other fascinating fallacies that deluded tens of thousands. "Should be read by everyone, scientist and non-scientist alike," R. T. Birge, Prof. Emeritus, Univ. of California; Former President, American Physical Society. Formerly titled, "In the Name of Science." Revised and enlarged edition. x + 365pp. 5⅜ x 8.
T394 Paperbound **$1.50**

THE STUDY OF THE HISTORY OF MATHEMATICS, THE STUDY OF THE HISTORY OF SCIENCE, G. Sarton. Two books bound as one. Both volumes are standard introductions to their fields by an eminent science historian. They discuss problems of historical research, teaching, pitfalls, other matters of interest to the historically oriented writer, teacher, or student. Both have extensive bibliographies. 10 illustrations. 188pp. 5⅜ x 8. T240 Paperbound **$1.25**

THE PRINCIPLES OF SCIENCE, W. S. Jevons. Unabridged reprinting of a milestone in the development of symbolic logic and other subjects concerning scientific methodology, probability, inferential validity, etc. Also describes Jevons' "logic machine," an early precursor of modern electronic calculators. Preface by E. Nagel. 839pp. 5⅜ x 8. S446 Paperbound **$2.98**

SCIENCE THEORY AND MAN, Erwin Schroedinger. Complete, unabridged reprinting of "Science and the Human Temperament" plus an additional essay "What is an Elementary Particle?" Nobel Laureate Schroedinger discusses many aspects of modern physics from novel points of view which provide unusual insights for both laymen and physicists. 192 pp. 5⅜ x 8.
T428 Paperbound **$1.35**

BRIDGES AND THEIR BUILDERS, D. B. Steinman & S. R. Watson. Information about ancient, medieval, modern bridges; how they were built; who built them; the structural principles employed; the materials they are built of; etc. Written by one of the world's leading authorities on bridge design and construction. New, revised, expanded edition. 23 photos; 26 line drawings, xvii + 401pp. 5⅜ x 8. T431 Paperbound **$1.95**

HISTORY OF MATHEMATICS, D. E. Smith. Most comprehensive non-technical history of math in English. In two volumes. Vol. I: A chronological examination of the growth of mathematics from primitive concepts up to 1900. Vol. II: The development of ideas in specific fields and areas, up through elementary calculus. The lives and works of over a thousand mathematicians are covered; thousands of specific historical problems and their solutions are clearly explained. Total of 510 illustrations, 1355pp. 5⅜ x 8. Set boxed in attractive container. T429, T430 Paperbound, the set **$5.00**

PHILOSOPHY AND THE PHYSICISTS, L. S. Stebbing. A philosopher examines the philosophical implications of modern science by posing a lively critical attack on the popular science expositions of Sir James Jeans and Arthur Eddington. xvi + 295pp. 5⅜ x 8.
T480 Paperbound **$1.65**

ON MATHEMATICS AND MATHEMATICIANS, R. E. Moritz. The first collection of quotations by and about mathematicians in English. 1140 anecdotes, aphorisms, definitions, speculations, etc. give both mathematicians and layman stimulating new insights into what mathematics is, and into the personalities of the great mathematicians from Archimedes to Euler, Gauss, Klein, Weierstrass. Invaluable to teachers, writers. Extensive cross index. 410pp. 5⅜ x 8.
T489 Paperbound **$1.95**

NATURAL SCIENCE, BIOLOGY, GEOLOGY, TRAVEL

A SHORT HISTORY OF ANATOMY AND PHYSIOLOGY FROM THE GREEKS TO HARVEY, C. Singer. A great medical historian's fascinating intermediate account of the slow advance of anatomical and physiological knowledge from pre-scientific times to Vesalius, Harvey. 139 unusually interesting illustrations. 221pp. 5⅜ x 8. T389 Paperbound **$1.75**

THE BEHAVIOUR AND SOCIAL LIFE OF HONEYBEES, Ronald Ribbands. The most comprehensive, lucid and authoritative book on bee habits, communication, duties, cell life, motivations, etc. "A MUST for every scientist, experimenter, and educator, and a happy and valuable selection for all interested in the honeybee," AMERICAN BEE JOURNAL. 690-item bibliography. 127 illus.; 11 photographic plates. 352pp. 5⅜ x 8⅜. S410 Clothbound **$4.50**

TRAVELS OF WILLIAM BARTRAM, edited by Mark Van Doren. One of the 18th century's most delightful books, and one of the few first-hand sources of information about American geography, natural history, and anthropology of American Indian tribes of the time. "The mind of a scientist with the soul of a poet," John Livingston Lowes. 13 original illustrations, maps. Introduction by Mark Van Doren. 448pp. 5⅜ x 8. T326 Paperbound **$2.00**

STUDIES ON THE STRUCTURE AND DEVELOPMENT OF VERTEBRATES, Edwin Goodrich. The definitive study of the skeleton, fins and limbs, head region, divisions of the body cavity, vascular, respiratory, excretory systems, etc., of vertebrates from fish to higher mammals, by the greatest comparative anatomist of recent times. "The standard textbook," JOURNAL OF ANATOMY. 754 illus. 69-page biographical study. 1186-item bibliography. 2 vols. Total of 906pp. 5⅜ x 8. Vol. I: S449 Paperbound **$2.50**
Vol. II: S450 Paperbound **$2.50**

DOVER BOOKS

THE BIRTH AND DEVELOPMENT OF THE GEOLOGICAL SCIENCES, F. D. Adams. The most complete and thorough history of the earth sciences in print. Covers over 300 geological thinkers and systems; treats fossils, theories of stone growth, paleontology, earthquakes, vulcanists vs. neptunists, odd theories, etc. 91 illustrations, including medieval, Renaissance wood cuts, etc. 632 footnotes and bibliographic notes. 511pp. 308pp. 5⅜ x 8.   T5 Paperbound **$2.00**

FROM MAGIC TO SCIENCE, Charles Singer. A close study of aspects of medical science from the Roman Empire through the Renaissance. The sections on early herbals, and "The Visions of Hildegarde of Bingen," are probably the best studies of these subjects available. 158 unusual classic and medieval illustrations. xxvii + 365pp. 5⅜ x 8.   T390 Paperbound **$2.00**

SAILING ALONE AROUND THE WORLD, Captain Joshua Slocum. Captain Slocum's personal account of his single-handed voyage around the world in a 34-foot boat he rebuilt himself. A classic of both seamanship and descriptive writing. "A nautical equivalent of Thoreau's account," Van Wyck Brooks. 67 illus. 308pp. 5⅜ x 8.   T326 Paperbound **$1.00**

TREES OF THE EASTERN AND CENTRAL UNITED STATES AND CANADA, W. M. Harlow. Standard middle-level guide designed to help you know the characteristics of Eastern trees and identify them at sight by means of an 8-page synoptic key. More than 600 drawings and photographs of twigs, leaves, fruit, other features. xiii + 288pp. 4⅝ x 6½.
T395 Paperbound **$1.35**

FRUIT KEY AND TWIG KEY ("Fruit Key to Northeastern Trees," "Twig Key to Deciduous Woody Plants of Eastern North America"), **W. M. Harlow.** Identify trees in fall, winter, spring. Easy-to-use, synoptic keys, with photographs of every twig and fruit identified. Covers 120 different fruits, 160 different twigs. Over 350 photos. Bibliographies. Glossaries. Total of 143pp. 5⅝ x 8⅜.   T511 Paperbound **$1.25**

INTRODUCTION TO THE STUDY OF EXPERIMENTAL MEDICINE, Claude Bernard. This classic records Bernard's far-reaching efforts to transform physiology into an exact science. It covers problems of vivisection, the limits of physiological experiment, hypotheses in medical experimentation, hundreds of others. Many of his own famous experiments on the liver, the pancreas, etc., are used as examples. Foreword by I. B. Cohen. xxv + 266pp. 5⅜ x 8.
T400 Paperbound **$1.50**

THE ORIGIN OF LIFE, A. I. Oparin. The first modern statement that life evolved from complex nitro-carbon compounds, carefully presented according to modern biochemical knowledge of primary colloids, organic molecules, etc. Begins with historical introduction to the problem of the origin of life. Bibliography. xxv + 270pp. 5⅜ x 8.   S213 Paperbound **$1.75**

A HISTORY OF ASTRONOMY FROM THALES TO KEPLER, J. L. E. Dreyer. The only work in English which provides a detailed picture of man's cosmological views from Egypt, Babylonia, Greece, and Alexandria to Copernicus, Tycho Brahe and Kepler. "Standard reference on Greek astronomy and the Copernican revolution," SKY AND TELESCOPE. Formerly called "A History of Planetary Systems From Thales to Kepler." Bibliography. 21 diagrams. xvii + 430pp. 5⅜ x 8.
S79 Paperbound **$1.98**

URANIUM PROSPECTING, H. L. Barnes. A professional geologist tells you what you need to know. Hundreds of facts about minerals, tests, detectors, sampling, assays, claiming, developing, government regulations, etc. Glossary of technical terms. Annotated bibliography. x + 117pp. 5⅜ x 8.   T309 Paperbound **$1.00**

DE RE METALLICA, Georgius Agricola. All 12 books of this 400 year old classic on metals and metal production, fully annotated, and containing all 289 of the 16th century woodcuts which made the original an artistic masterpiece. A superb gift for geologists, engineers, libraries, artists, historians. Translated by Herbert Hoover & L. H. Hoover. Bibliography, survey of ancient authors. 289 illustrations of the excavating, assaying, smelting, refining, and countless other metal production operations described in the text. 672pp. 6¾ x 10¾. Deluxe library edition.   S6 Clothbound **$10.00**

DE MAGNETE, William Gilbert. A landmark of science by the man who first used the word "electricity," distinguished between static electricity and magnetism, and founded a new science. P. F. Mottelay translation. 90 figures. lix + 368pp. 5⅜ x 8.   S470 Paperbound **$2.00**

THE AUTOBIOGRAPHY OF CHARLES DARWIN AND SELECTED LETTERS, Francis Darwin, ed. Fascinating documents on Darwin's early life, the voyage of the "Beagle," the discovery of evolution, Darwin's thought on mimicry, plant development, vivisection, evolution, many other subjects Letters to Henslow, Lyell, Hooker, Wallace, Kingsley, etc. Appendix. 365pp. 5⅜ x 8.   T479 Paperbound **$1.65**

A WAY OF LIFE AND OTHER SELECTED WRITINGS OF SIR WILLIAM OSLER. 16 of the great physician, teacher and humanist's most inspiring writings on a practical philosophy of life, science and the humanities, and the history of medicine. 5 photographs. Introduction by G. L. Keynes, M.D., F.R.C.S. xx + 278pp. 5⅜ x 8.   T488 Paperbound **$1.50**

LITERATURE

WORLD DRAMA, B. H. Clark. 46 plays from Ancient Greece, Rome, to India, China, Japan. Plays by Aeschylus, Sophocles, Euripides, Aristophanes, Plautus, Marlowe, Jonson, Farquhar, Goldsmith, Cervantes, Molière, Dumas, Goethe, Schiller, Ibsen, many others. One of the most comprehensive collections of important plays from all literature available in English. Over ⅓ of this material is unavailable in any other current edition. Reading lists. 2 volumes. Total of 1364pp. 5⅜ x 8.
Vol. I, T57 Paperbound **$2.00**
Vol. II, T59 Paperbound **$2.00**

MASTERS OF THE DRAMA, John Gassner. The most comprehensive history of the drama in print. Covers more than 800 dramatists and over 2000 plays from the Greeks to modern Western, Near Eastern, Oriental drama. Plot summaries, theatre history, etc. "Best of its kind in English," NEW REPUBLIC. 35 pages of bibliography. 77 photos and drawings. Deluxe edition. xxii + 890pp. 5⅜ x 8.
T100 Clothbound **$5.95**

THE DRAMA OF LUIGI PIRANDELLO, D. Vittorini. All 38 of Pirandello's plays (to 1935) summarized and analyzed in terms of symbolic techniques, plot structure, etc. The only authorized work. Foreword by Pirandello. Biography. Bibliography. xiii + 350pp. 5⅜ x 8.
T435 Paperbound **$1.98**

ARISTOTLE'S THEORY OF POETRY AND THE FINE ARTS, S. H. Butcher, ed. The celebrated "Butcher translation" faced page by page with the Greek text; Butcher's 300-page introduction to Greek poetic, dramatic thought. Modern Aristotelian criticism discussed by John Gassner. lxxvi + 421pp. 5⅜ x 8.
T42 Paperbound **$2.00**

EUGENE O'NEILL: THE MAN AND HIS PLAYS, B. H. Clark. The first published source-book on O'Neill's life and work. Analyzes each play from the early THE WEB up to THE ICEMAN COMETH. Supplies much information about environmental and dramatic influences. ix + 182pp. 5⅜ x 8.
T379 Paperbound **$1.25**

INTRODUCTION TO ENGLISH LITERATURE, B. Dobrée, ed. Most compendious literary aid in its price range. Extensive, categorized bibliography (with entries up to 1949) of more than 5,000 poets, dramatists, novelists, as well as historians, philosophers, economists, religious writers, travellers, and scientists of literary stature. Information about manuscripts, important biographical data. Critical, historical, background works not simply listed, but evaluated. Each volume also contains a long introduction to the period it covers.

Vol. I: **THE BEGINNINGS OF ENGLISH LITERATURE TO SKELTON, 1509, W. L. Renwick. H. Orton.** 450pp. 5⅛ x 7⅛.
T75 Clothbound **$3.50**
Vol. II: **THE ENGLISH RENAISSANCE, 1510-1688, V. de Sola Pinto.** 381pp. 5⅛ x 7⅛.
T76 Clothbound **$3.50**
Vol. III: **THE AUGUSTANS AND ROMANTICS, 1689-1830, H. Dyson, J. Butt.** 320pp. 5⅛ x 7⅛.
T77 Clothbound **$3.50**
Vol. IV: **THE VICTORIANS AND AFTER, 1830-1914, E. Batho, B. Dobrée.** 360pp. 5⅛ x 7⅛.
T78 Clothbound **$3.50**

EPIC AND ROMANCE, W. P. Ker. The standard survey of Medieval epic and romance by a foremost authority on Medieval literature. Covers historical background, plot, literary analysis, significance of Teutonic epics, Icelandic sagas, Beowulf, French chansons de geste, the Niebelungenlied, Arthurian romances, much more. 422pp. 5⅜ x 8.
T355 Paperbound **$1.95**

THE HEART OF EMERSON'S JOURNALS, Bliss Perry, ed. Emerson's most intimate thoughts, impressions, records of conversations with Channing, Hawthorne, Thoreau, etc., carefully chosen from the 10 volumes of The Journals. "The essays do not reveal the power of Emerson's mind . . . as do these hasty and informal writings," N. Y. TIMES. Preface by B. Perry. 370pp. 5⅜ x 8.
T447 Paperbound **$1.85**

A SOURCE BOOK IN THEATRICAL HISTORY, A. M. Nagler. (Formerly, "Sources of Theatrical History.") Over 300 selected passages by contemporary observers tell about styles of acting, direction, make-up, scene designing, etc., in the theatre's great periods from ancient Greece to the Théâtre Libre. "Indispensable complement to the study of drama," EDUCATIONAL THEATRE JOURNAL. Prof. Nagler, Yale Univ. School of Drama, also supplies notes, references. 85 illustrations. 611pp. 5⅜ x 8.
T515 Paperbound **$2.75**

THE ART OF THE STORY-TELLER, M. L. Shedlock. Regarded as the finest, most helpful book on telling stories to children, by a great story-teller. How to catch, hold, recapture attention; how to choose material; many other aspects. Also includes: a 99-page selection of Miss Shedlock's most successful stories; extensive bibliography of other stories. xxi + 320pp. 5⅜ x 8.
T245 Clothbound **$3.50**

THE DEVIL'S DICTIONARY, Ambrose Bierce. Over 1000 short, ironic definitions in alphabetical order, by America's greatest satirist in the classical tradition. "Some of the most gorgeous witticisms in the English language," H. L. Mencken. 144pp. 5⅜ x 8.
T487 Paperbound **$1.00**

MUSIC

A DICTIONARY OF HYMNOLOGY, John Julian. More than 30,000 entries on individual hymns, their authorship, textual variations, location of texts, dates and circumstances of composition, denominational and ritual usages, the biographies of more than 9,000 hymn writers, essays on important topics such as children's hymns and Christmas carols, and hundreds of thousands of other important facts about hymns which are virtually impossible to find anywhere else. Convenient alphabetical listing, and a 200-page double-columned index of first lines enable you to track down virtually any hymn ever written. Total of 1786pp. 6¼ x 9¼. 2 volumes. T133. The Set, Clothbound **$15.00**

STRUCTURAL HEARING, TONAL COHERENCE IN MUSIC, Felix Salzer. Extends the well-known Schenker approach to include modern music, music of the middle ages, and Renaissance music. Explores the phenomenon of tonal organization by discussing more than 500 compositions, and offers unusual new insights into the theory of composition and musical relationships. "The foundation on which all teaching in music theory has been based at this college," Leopold Mannes, President, The Mannes College of Music. Total of 658pp. 6½ x 9¼. 2 volumes. S418 The set, Clothbound **$8.00**

A GENERAL HISTORY OF MUSIC, Charles Burney. The complete history of music from the Greeks up to 1789 by the 18th century musical historian who personally knew the great Baroque composers. Covers sacred and secular, vocal and instrumental, operatic and symphonic music; treats theory, notation, forms, instruments; discusses composers, performers, important works. Invaluable as a source of information on the period for students, historians, musicians. "Surprisingly few of Burney's statements have been invalidated by modern research . . . still of great value," NEW YORK TIMES. Edited and corrected by Frank Mercer. 35 figures. 1915pp. 5½ x 8½. 2 volumes. T36 The set, Clothbound **$12.50**

JOHANN SEBASTIAN BACH, Phillip Spitta. Recognized as one of the greatest accomplishments of musical scholarship and far and away the definitive coverage of Bach's works. Hundreds of individual pieces are analyzed. Major works, such as the B Minor Mass and the St. Matthew Passion are examined in minute detail. Spitta also deals with the works of Buxtehude, Pachelbel, and others of the period. Can be read with profit even by those without a knowledge of the technicalities of musical composition. "Unchallenged as the last word on one of the supreme geniuses of music," John Barkham, SATURDAY REVIEW SYNDICATE. Total of 1819pp. 5⅜ x 8. 2 volumes. T252 The set, Clothbound **$10.00**

HISTORY

THE IDEA OF PROGRESS, J. B. Bury. Prof. Bury traces the evolution of a central concept of Western civilization in Greek, Roman, Medieval, and Renaissance thought to its flowering in the 17th and 18th centuries. Introduction by Charles Beard. xl + 357pp. 5⅜ x 8.
T39 Clothbound **$3.95**
T40 Paperbound **$1.95**

THE ANCIENT GREEK HISTORIANS, J. B. Bury. Greek historians such as Herodotus, Thucydides, Xenophon; Roman historians such as Tacitus, Caesar, Livy; scores of others fully analyzed in terms of sources, concepts, influences, etc., by a great scholar and historian. 291pp. 5⅜ x 8. T397 Paperbound **$1.50**

HISTORY OF THE LATER ROMAN EMPIRE, J. B. Bury. The standard work on the Byzantine Empire from 395 A.D. to the death of Justinian in 565 A.D., by the leading Byzantine scholar of our time. Covers political, social, cultural, theological, military history. Quotes contemporary documents extensively. "Most unlikely that it will ever be superseded," Glanville Downey, Dumbarton Oaks Research Library. Genealogical tables. 5 maps. Bibliography. 2 vols. Total of 965pp. 5⅜ x 8. T398, T399 Paperbound, the set **$4.00**

GARDNER'S PHOTOGRAPHIC SKETCH BOOK OF THE CIVIL WAR, Alexander Gardner. One of the rarest and most valuable Civil War photographic collections exactly reproduced for the first time since 1866. Scenes of Manassas, Bull Run, Harper's Ferry, Appomattox, Mechanicsville, Fredericksburg, Gettysburg, etc.; battle ruins, prisons, arsenals, a slave pen, fortifications; Lincoln on the field, officers, men, corpses. By one of the most famous pioneers in documentary photography. Original copies of the "Sketch Book" sold for $425 in 1952. Introduction by E. Bleiler. 100 full-page 7 x 10 photographs (original size). 244pp. 10¾ x 8½.
T476 Clothbound **$6.00**

THE WORLD'S GREAT SPEECHES, L. Copeland and L. Lamm, eds. 255 speeches from Pericles to Churchill, Dylan Thomas. Invaluable as a guide to speakers; fascinating as history past and present; a source of much difficult-to-find material. Includes an extensive section of informal and humorous speeches. 3 indices: Topic, Author, Nation. xx + 745pp. 5⅜ x 8.
T468 Paperbound **$2.49**

FOUNDERS OF THE MIDDLE AGES, E. K. Rand. The best non-technical discussion of the transformation of Latin paganism into medieval civilization. Tertullian, Gregory, Jerome, Boethius, Augustine, the Neoplatonists, other crucial figures, philosophies examined. Excellent for the intelligent non-specialist. "Extraordinarily accurate," Richard McKeon, THE NATION. ix + 365pp. 5⅜ x 8. T369 Paperbound **$1.85**

THE POLITICAL THOUGHT OF PLATO AND ARISTOTLE, Ernest Barker. The standard, comprehensive exposition of Greek political thought. Covers every aspect of the "Republic" and the "Politics" as well as minor writings, other philosophers, theorists of the period, and the later history of Greek political thought. Unabridged edition. 584pp. 5⅜ x 8.
T521 Paperbound **$1.85**

PHILOSOPHY

THE GIFT OF LANGUAGE, M. Schlauch. (Formerly, "The Gift of Tongues.") A sound, middle-level treatment of linguistic families, word histories, grammatical processes, semantics, language taboos, word-coining of Joyce, Cummings, Stein, etc. 232 bibliographical notes. 350pp. 5⅜ x 8.
T243 Paperbound **$1.85**

THE PHILOSOPHY OF HEGEL, W. T. Stace. The first work in English to give a complete and connected view of Hegel's entire system. Especially valuable to those who do not have time to study the highly complicated original texts, yet want an accurate presentation by a most reputable scholar of one of the most influential 19th century thinkers. Includes a 14 x 20 fold-out chart of Hegelian system. 536pp. 5⅜ x 8.
T254 Paperbound **$2.00**

ARISTOTLE, A. E. Taylor. A lucid, non-technical account of Aristotle written by a foremost Platonist. Covers life and works; thought on matter, form, causes, logic, God, physics, metaphysics, etc. Bibliography. New index compiled for this edition. 128pp. 5⅜ x 8.
T280 Paperbound **$1.00**

GUIDE TO PHILOSOPHY, C. E. M. Joad. This basic work describes the major philosophic problems and evaluates the answers propounded by great philosophers from the Greeks to Whitehead, Russell. "The finest introduction," BOSTON TRANSCRIPT. Bibliography, 592pp. 5⅜ x 8.
T297 Paperbound **$2.00**

LANGUAGE AND MYTH, E. Cassirer. Cassirer's brilliant demonstration that beneath both language and myth lies an unconscious "grammar" of experience whose categories and canons are not those of logical thought. Introduction and translation by Susanne Langer. Index. x + 103pp. 5⅜ x 8.
T51 Paperbound **$1.25**

SUBSTANCE AND FUNCTION, EINSTEIN'S THEORY OF RELATIVITY, E. Cassirer. This double volume contains the German philosopher's profound philosophical formulation of the differences between traditional logic and the new logic of science. Number, space, energy, relativity, many other topics are treated in detail. Authorized translation by W. C. and M. C. Swabey. xii + 465pp. 5⅜ x 8.
T50 Paperbound **$2.00**

THE PHILOSOPHICAL WORKS OF DESCARTES. The definitive English edition, in two volumes, of all major philosophical works and letters of René Descartes, father of modern philosophy of knowledge and science. Translated by E. S. Haldane and G. Ross. Introductory notes. Total of 842pp. 5⅜ x 8.
T71 Vol. 1, Paperbound **$2.00**
T72 Vol. 2, Paperbound **$2.00**

ESSAYS IN EXPERIMENTAL LOGIC, J. Dewey. Based upon Dewey's theory that knowledge implies a judgment which in turn implies an inquiry, these papers consider such topics as the thought of Bertrand Russell, pragmatism, the logic of values, antecedents of thought, data and meanings. 452pp. 5⅜ x 8.
T73 Paperbound **$1.95**

THE PHILOSOPHY OF HISTORY, G. W. F. Hegel. This classic of Western thought is Hegel's detailed formulation of the thesis that history is not chance but a rational process, the realization of the Spirit of Freedom. Translated and introduced by J. Sibree. Introduction by C. Hegel. Special introduction for this edition by Prof. Carl Friedrich, Harvard University. xxxix + 447pp. 5⅜ x 8.
T112 Paperbound **$1.85**

THE WILL TO BELIEVE and HUMAN IMMORTALITY, W. James. Two of James's most profound investigations of human belief in God and immortality, bound as one volume. Both are powerful expressions of James's views on chance vs. determinism, pluralism vs. monism, will and intellect, arguments for survival after death, etc. Two prefaces. 429pp. 5⅜ x 8.
T294 Clothbound **$3.75**
T291 Paperbound **$1.65**

INTRODUCTION TO SYMBOLIC LOGIC, S. Langer. A lucid, general introduction to modern logic, covering forms, classes, the use of symbols, the calculus of propositions, the Boole-Schroeder and the Russell-Whitehead systems, etc. "One of the clearest and simplest introductions," MATHEMATICS GAZETTE. Second, enlarged, revised edition. 368pp. 5⅜ x 8.
S164 Paperbound **$1.75**

MIND AND THE WORLD-ORDER, C. I. Lewis. Building upon the work of Peirce, James, and Dewey, Professor Lewis outlines a theory of knowledge in terms of "conceptual pragmatism," and demonstrates why the traditional understanding of the a priori must be abandoned. Appendices. xiv + 446pp. 5⅜ x 8.
T359 Paperbound **$1.95**

THE GUIDE FOR THE PERPLEXED. M. Maimonides One of the great philosophical works of all time, Maimonides' formulation of the meeting-ground between Old Testament and Aristotelian thought is essential to anyone interested in Jewish, Christian, and Moslem thought in the Middle Ages. 2nd revised edition of the Friedländer translation. Extensive introduction. lix + 414pp. 5⅜ x 8.
T351 Paperbound **$1.85**

DOVER BOOKS

THE PHILOSOPHICAL WRITINGS OF PEIRCE, J. Buchler, ed. (Formerly, "The Philosophy of Peirce.") This carefully integrated selection of Peirce's papers is considered the best coverage of the complete thought of one of the greatest philosophers of modern times. Covers Peirce's work on the theory of signs, pragmatism, epistemology, symbolic logic, the scientific method, chance, etc. xvi + 386pp. 5 ⅜ x 8. 　　　　　　　　T216 Clothbound **$5.00**
　　　　　　　　　　　　　　　　　　　　　　　　　　　　　　T217 Paperbound **$1.95**

HISTORY OF ANCIENT PHILOSOPHY, W. Windelband. Considered the clearest survey of Greek and Roman philosophy. Examines Thales, Anaximander, Anaximenes, Heraclitus, the Eleatics, Empedocles, the Pythagoreans, the Sophists, Socrates, Democritus, Stoics, Epicureans, Sceptics, Neo-platonists, etc. 50 pages on Plato; 70 on Aristotle. 2nd German edition tr. by H. E. Cushman. xv + 393pp. 5⅜ x 8. 　　　　　　　　　　　　　　T357 Paperbound **$1.75**

INTRODUCTION TO SYMBOLIC LOGIC AND ITS APPLICATIONS, R. Carnap. A comprehensive, rigorous introduction to modern logic by perhaps its greatest living master. Includes demonstrations of applications in mathematics, physics, biology. "Of the rank of a masterpiece," Z. für Mathematik und ihre Grenzgebiete. Over 300 exercises. xvi + 241pp. 5⅜ x 8. 　　　　　　　　　　　　　　　　　　　Clothbound **$4.00**
　　　　　　　　　　　　　　　　　　　　　　　　　　　　S453 Paperbound **$1.85**

SCEPTICISM AND ANIMAL FAITH, G. Santayana. Santayana's unusually lucid exposition of the difference between the independent existence of objects and the essence our mind attributes to them, and of the necessity of scepticism as a form of belief and animal faith as a necessary condition of knowledge. Discusses belief, memory, intuition, symbols, etc. xii + 314pp. 5⅜ x 8. 　　　　　　　　　　　　　　　　　　T235 Clothbound **$3.50**
　　　　　　　　　　　　　　　　　　　　　　　　　　　　T236 Paperbound **$1.50**

THE ANALYSIS OF MATTER, B. Russell. With his usual brilliance, Russell analyzes physics, causality, scientific inference, Weyl's theory, tensors, invariants, periodicity, etc. in order to discover the basic concepts of scientific thought about matter. "Most thorough treatment of the subject," THE NATION. Introduction. 8 figures. viii + 408pp. 5⅜ x 8.
　　　　　　　　　　　　　　　　　　　　　　　　　　　　T231 Paperbound **$1.95**

THE SENSE OF BEAUTY, G. Santayana. This important philosophical study of why, when, and how beauty appears, and what conditions must be fulfilled, is in itself a revelation of the beauty of language. "It is doubtful if a better treatment of the subject has since appeared," PEABODY JOURNAL. ix + 275pp. 5⅜ x 8. 　　　　　　T238 Paperbound **$1.00**

THE CHIEF WORKS OF SPINOZA. In two volumes. Vol. I: The Theologico-Political Treatise and the Political Treatise. Vol. II: On the Improvement of Understanding, The Ethics, and Selected Letters. The permanent and enduring ideas in these works on God, the universe, religion, society, etc., have had tremendous impact on later philosophical works. Introduction. Total of 862pp. 5⅜ x 8. 　　　　　　　　T249 Vol. I, Paperbound **$1.50**
　　　　　　　　　　　　　　　　　　　　　　　　T250 Vol. II, Paperbound **$1.50**

TRAGIC SENSE OF LIFE, M. de Unamuno. The acknowledged masterpiece of one of Spain's most influential thinkers. Between the despair at the inevitable death of man and all his works, and the desire for immortality, Unamuno finds a "saving incertitude." Called "a masterpiece," by the ENCYCLOPAEDIA BRITANNICA. xxx + 332pp. 5⅜ x 8.
　　　　　　　　　　　　　　　　　　　　　　　　　　　　T257 Paperbound **$1.95**

EXPERIENCE AND NATURE, John Dewey. The enlarged, revised edition of the Paul Carus lectures (1925). One of Dewey's clearest presentations of the philosophy of empirical naturalism which reestablishes the continuity between "inner" experience and "outer" nature. These lectures are among the most significant ever delivered by an American philosopher. 457pp. 5⅜ x 8. 　　　　　　　　　　　　　　　　　T471 Paperbound **$1.85**

PHILOSOPHY AND CIVILIZATION IN THE MIDDLE AGES, M. de Wulf. A semi-popular survey of medieval intellectual life, religion, philosophy, science, the arts, etc. that covers feudalism vs. Catholicism, rise of the universities, mendicant orders, and similar topics. Bibliography. viii + 320pp. 5⅜ x 8. 　　　　　　　　　　　　T284 Paperbound **$1.75**

AN INTRODUCTION TO SCHOLASTIC PHILOSOPHY, M. de Wulf. (Formerly, "Scholasticism Old and New.") Prof. de Wulf covers the central scholastic tradition from St. Anselm, Albertus Magnus, Thomas Aquinas, up to Suarez in the 17th century; and then treats the modern revival of scholasticism, the Louvain position, relations with Kantianism and positivism, etc. xvi + 271pp. 5⅜ x 8. 　　　　　　　　　　T296 Clothbound **$3.50**
　　　　　　　　　　　　　　　　　　　　　　　　　　　　T283 Paperbound **$1.75**

A HISTORY OF MODERN PHILOSOPHY, H. Höffding. An exceptionally clear and detailed coverage of Western philosophy from the Renaissance to the end of the 19th century. Both major and minor figures are examined in terms of theory of knowledge, logic, cosmology, psychology. Covers Pomponazzi, Bodin, Boehme, Telesius, Bruno, Copernicus, Descartes, Spinoza, Hobbes, Locke, Hume, Kant, Fichte, Schopenhauer, Mill, Spencer, Langer, scores of others. A standard reference work. 2 volumes. Total of 1159pp. 5⅜ x 8. 　　T117 Vol. 1, Paperbound **$2.00**
　　　　　　　　　　　　　　　　　　　　　　　　T118 Vol. 2, Paperbound **$2.00**

LANGUAGE, TRUTH AND LOGIC, A. J. Ayer. The first full-length development of Logical Positivism in English. Building on the work of Schlick, Russell, Carnap, and the Vienna school, Ayer presents the tenets of one of the most important systems of modern philosophical thought. 160pp. 5⅜ x 8. 　　　　　　　　　　　T10 Paperbound **$1.25**

ORIENTALIA AND RELIGION

THE MYSTERIES OF MITHRA, F. Cumont. The great Belgian scholar's definitive study of the Persian mystery religion that almost vanquished Christianity in the ideological struggle for the Roman Empire. A masterpiece of scholarly detection that reconstructs secret doctrines, organization, rites. Mithraic art is discussed and analyzed. 70 illus. 239pp. 5⅜ x 8.
T323 Paperbound **$1.85**

CHRISTIAN AND ORIENTAL PHILOSOPHY OF ART. A. K. Coomaraswamy. The late art historian and orientalist discusses artistic symbolism, the role of traditional culture in enriching art, medieval art, folklore, philosophy of art, other similar topics. Bibliography. 148pp. 5⅜ x 8.
T378 Paperbound **$1.25**

TRANSFORMATION OF NATURE IN ART, A. K. Coomaraswamy. A basic work on Asiatic religious art. Includes discussions of religious art in Asia and Medieval Europe (exemplified by Meister Eckhart), the origin and use of images in Indian art, Indian Medieval aesthetic manuals, and other fascinating, little known topics. Glossaries of Sanskrit and Chinese terms. Bibliography. 41pp. of notes. 245pp. 5⅜ x 8.
T368 Paperbound **$1.75**

ORIENTAL RELIGIONS IN ROMAN PAGANISM, F. Cumont. This well-known study treats the ecstatic cults of Syria and Phrygia (Cybele, Attis, Adonis, their orgies and mutilatory rites); the mysteries of Egypt (Serapis, Isis, Osiris); Persian dualism; Mithraic cults; Hermes Trismegistus, Ishtar, Astarte, etc. and their influence on the religious thought of the Roman Empire. Introduction. 55pp. of notes; extensive bibliography. xxiv + 298pp. 5⅜ x 8.
T321 Paperbound **$1.75**

ANTHROPOLOGY, SOCIOLOGY, AND PSYCHOLOGY

PRIMITIVE MAN AS PHILOSOPHER, P. Radin. A standard anthropological work based on Radin's investigations of the Winnebago, Maori, Batak, Zuni, other primitive tribes. Describes primitive thought on the purpose of life, marital relations, death, personality, gods, etc. Extensive selections of original primitive documents. Bibliography. xviii + 420pp. 5⅜ x 8.
T392 Paperbound **$2.00**

PRIMITIVE RELIGION, P. Radin. Radin's thoroughgoing treatment of supernatural beliefs, shamanism, initiations, religious expression, etc. in primitive societies. Arunta, Ashanti, Aztec, Bushman, Crow, Fijian, many other tribes examined. "Excellent," NATURE. New preface by the author. Bibliographic notes. x + 322pp. 5⅜ x 8.   T393 Paperbound **$1.85**

SEX IN PSYCHO-ANALYSIS, S. Ferenczi. (Formerly, "Contributions to Psycho-analysis.") 14 selected papers on impotence, transference, analysis and children, dreams, obscene words, homosexuality, paranoia, etc. by an associate of Freud. Also included: THE DEVELOPMENT OF PSYCHO-ANALYSIS, by Ferenczi and Otto Rank. Two books bound as one. Total of 406pp. 5⅜ x 8.   T324 Paperbound **$1.85**

THE PRINCIPLES OF PSYCHOLOGY, William James. The complete text of the famous "long course," one of the great books of Western thought. An almost incredible amount of information about psychological processes, the stream of consciousness, habit, time perception, memory, emotions, reason, consciousness of self, abnormal phenomena, and similar topics. Based on James's own discoveries integrated with the work of Descartes, Locke, Hume, Royce, Wundt, Berkeley, Lotse, Herbart, scores of others. "A classic of interpretation," PSYCHIATRIC QUARTERLY. 94 illus. 1408pp. 2 volumes. 5⅜ x 8.
T381 Vol. 1, Paperbound **$2.50**
T382 Vol. 2, Paperbound **$2.50**

THE POLISH PEASANT IN EUROPE AND AMERICA, W. I. Thomas, F. Znaniecki. Monumental sociological study of peasant primary groups (family and community) and the disruptions produced by a new industrial system and emigration to America, by two of the foremost sociologists of recent times. One of the most important works in sociological thought. Includes hundreds of pages of primary documentation; point by point analysis of causes of social decay, breakdown of morality, crime, drunkenness, prostitution, etc. 2nd revised edition. 2 volumes. Total of 2250pp. 6 x 9.   T478 2 volume set, Clothbound **$12.50**

FOLKWAYS, W. G. Sumner. The great Yale sociologist's detailed exposition of thousands of social, sexual, and religious customs in hundreds of cultures from ancient Greece to Modern Western societies. Preface by A. G. Keller. Introduction by William Lyon Phelps. 705pp. 5⅜ x 8.   S508 Paperbound **$2.49**

BEYOND PSYCHOLOGY, Otto Rank. The author, an early associate of Freud, uses psychoanalytic techniques of myth-analysis to explore ultimates of human existence. Treats love, immortality, the soul, sexual identity, kingship, sources of state power, many other topics which illuminate the irrational basis of human existence. 291pp. 5⅜ x 8.   T485 Paperbound **$1.75**

ILLUSIONS AND DELUSIONS OF THE SUPERNATURAL AND THE OCCULT, D. H. Rawcliffe. A rational, scientific examination of crystal gazing, automatic writing, table turning, stigmata, the Indian rope trick, dowsing, telepathy, clairvoyance, ghosts, ESP, PK, thousands of other supposedly occult phenomena. Originally titled "The Psychology of the Occult." 14 illustrations. 551pp. 5⅜ x 8.   T503 Paperbound **$2.00**

DOVER BOOKS

YOGA: A SCIENTIFIC EVALUATION, Kovoor T. Behanan. A scientific study of the physiological and psychological effects of Yoga discipline, written under the auspices of the Yale University Institute of Human Relations. Foreword by W. A. Miles, Yale Univ. 17 photographs. 290pp. 5⅜ x 8. T505 Paperbound **$1.65**

HOAXES, C. D. MacDougall. Delightful, entertaining, yet scholarly exposition of how hoaxes start, why they succeed, documented with stories of hundreds of the most famous hoaxes. "A stupendous collection . . . and shrewd analysis, "NEW YORKER. New, revised edition. 54 photographs. 320pp. 5⅜ x 8. T465 Paperbound **$1.75**

CREATIVE POWER: THE EDUCATION OF YOUTH IN THE CREATIVE ARTS, Hughes Mearns. Named by the National Education Association as one of the 20 foremost books on education in recent times. Tells how to help children express themselves in drama, poetry, music, art, develop latent creative power. Should be read by every parent, teacher. New, enlarged, revised edition. Introduction. 272pp. 5⅜ x 8. T490 Paperbound **$1.50**

LANGUAGES

NEW RUSSIAN-ENGLISH, ENGLISH-RUSSIAN DICTIONARY, M. A. O'Brien. Over- 70,000 entries in new orthography! Idiomatic usages, colloquialisms. One of the few dictionaries that indicate accent changes in conjugation and declension. "One of the best," Prof. E. J. Simmons, Cornell. First names, geographical terms, bibliography, many other features. 738pp. 4½ x 6¼. T208 Paperbound **$2.00**

MONEY CONVERTER AND TIPPING GUIDE FOR EUROPEAN TRAVEL, C. Vomacka. Invaluable, handy source of currency regulations, conversion tables, tipping rules, postal rates, much other travel information for every European country plus Israel, Egypt and Turkey. 128pp. 3½ x 5¼. T260 Paperbound **60¢**

MONEY CONVERTER AND TIPPING GUIDE FOR TRAVEL IN THE AMERICAS (including the United States and Canada), **C. Vomacka.** The information you need for informed and confident travel in the Americas: money conversion tables, tipping guide, postal, telephone rates, etc. 128pp. 3½ x 5¼. T261 Paperbound **65¢**

DUTCH-ENGLISH, ENGLISH-DUTCH DICTIONARY, F. G. Renier. The most convenient, practical Dutch-English dictionary on the market. New orthography. More than 60,000 entries: idioms, compounds, technical terms, etc. Gender of nouns indicated. xviii + 571pp. 5½ x 6¼. T224 Clothbound **$2.50**

LEARN DUTCH!, F. G. Renier. The most satisfactory and easily-used grammar of modern Dutch. Used and recommended by the Fulbright Committee in the Netherlands. Over 1200 simple exercises lead to mastery of spoken and written Dutch. Dutch-English, English-Dutch vocabularies. 181pp. 4¼ x 7¼. T441 Clothbound **$1.75**

PHRASE AND SENTENCE DICTIONARY OF SPOKEN RUSSIAN, English-Russian, Russian-English. Based on phrases and complete sentences, rather than isolated words; recognized as one of the best methods of learning the idiomatic speech of a country. Over 11,500 entries, indexed by single words, with more than 32,000 English and Russian sentences and phrases, in immediately usable form. Probably the largest list ever published. Shows accent changes in conjugation and declension; irregular forms listed in both alphabetical place and under main form of word. 15,000 word introduction covering Russian sounds, writing, grammar, syntax. 15-page appendix of geographical names, money, important signs, given names, foods, special Soviet terms, etc. Travellers, businessmen, students, government employees have found this their best source for Russian expressions. Originally published as U.S. Government Technical Manual TM 30-944. iv + 573pp. 5⅝ x 8⅜. T496 Paperbound **$2.75**

PHRASE AND SENTENCE DICTIONARY OF SPOKEN SPANISH, Spanish-English, English-Spanish. Compiled from spoken Spanish, emphasizing idiom and colloquial usage in both Castilian and Latin-American. More than 16,000 entries containing over 25,000 idioms—the largest list of idiomatic constructions ever published. Complete sentences given, indexed under single words —language in immediately usable form, for travellers, businessmen, students, etc. 25-page introduction provides rapid survey of sounds, grammar, syntax, with full consideration of irregular verbs. Especially apt in modern treatment of phrases and structure. 17-page glossary gives translations of geographical names, money values, numbers, national holidays, important street signs, useful expressions of high frequency, plus unique 7-page glossary of Spanish and Spanish-American foods and dishes. Originally published as U.S. Government Technical Manual TM 30-900. iv + 513pp. 5⅝ x 8⅜. T495 Paperbound **$1.75**

SAY IT language phrase books

"SAY IT" in the foreign language of your choice! We have sold over ½ million copies of these popular, useful language books. They will not make you an expert linguist overnight, but they do cover most practical matters of everyday life abroad.

Over 1000 useful phrases, expressions, with additional variants, substitutions.

Modern! Useful! Hundreds of phrases not available in other texts: "Nylon," "air-conditioned," etc.

The ONLY inexpensive phrase book **completely indexed.** Everything is available at a flip of your finger, ready for use.

Prepared by native linguists, travel experts.

Based on years of travel experience abroad.

This handy phrase book may be used by itself, or it may supplement any other text or course; it provides a living element. Used by many colleges and institutions: Hunter College; Barnard College; Army Ordnance School, Aberdeen; and many others.

Available, 1 book per language:

Danish (T818) 75¢	**Italian** (T806) 60¢
Dutch T(817) 75¢	**Japanese** (T807) 60¢
English (for German-speaking people) (T801) 60¢	**Norwegian** (T814) 75¢
English (for Italian-speaking people) (T816) 60¢	**Russian** (T810) 75¢
English (for Spanish-speaking people) (T802) 60¢	**Spanish** (T811) 60¢
Esperanto (T820) 75¢	**Turkish** (T821) 75¢
French (T803) 60¢	**Yiddish** (T815) 75¢
German (T804) 60¢	**Swedish** (T812) 75¢
Modern Greek (T813) 75¢	**Polish** (T808) 75¢
Hebrew (T805) 60¢	**Portuguese** (T809) 75¢

LISTEN & LEARN language record sets

LISTEN & LEARN is the only language record course designed especially to meet your travel needs, or help you learn essential foreign language quickly by yourself, or in conjunction with any school course, by means of the automatic association method. Each set contains three 33⅓ rpm long- playing records — 1½ hours of recorded speech by eminent native speakers who are professors at Columbia, N.Y.U., Queens College and other leading universities. The sets are priced far below other sets of similar quality, yet they contain many special features not found in other record sets:

* Over 800 selected phrases and sentences, a basic vocabulary of over 3200 words.
* Both English and foreign language recorded; with a pause for your repetition.
* Designed for persons with limited time; no time wasted on material you cannot use immediately.
* Living, modern expressions that answer modern needs: drugstore items, "air-conditioned," etc.
* 128-196 page manuals contain everything on the records, plus simple pronunciation guides.
* Manual is fully indexed; find the phrase you want instantly.
* High fidelity recording—equal to any records costing up to $6 each.

The phrases on these records cover 41 different categories useful to the traveller or student interested in learning the living, spoken language: greetings, introductions, making yourself understood, passing customs, planes, trains, boats, buses, taxis, nightclubs, restaurants, menu items, sports, concerts, cameras, automobile travel, repairs, drugstores, doctors, dentists, medicines, barber shops, beauty parlors, laundries, many, many more.

"Excellent . . . among the very best on the market," Prof. Mario Pei, Dept. of Romance Languages, Columbia University. "Inexpensive and well-done . . . an ideal present," CHICAGO SUNDAY TRIBUNE. "More genuinely helpful than anything of its kind which I have previously encountered," Sidney Clark, well-known author of "ALL THE BEST" travel books. Each set contains 3 33⅓ rpm pure vinyl records, 128- 196 page with full record text, and album. One language per set. LISTEN & LEARN record sets are now available in—

FRENCH	the set $4.95		**GERMAN**	the set $4.95
ITALIAN	the set $4.95		**SPANISH**	the set $4.95
RUSSIAN	the set $5.95		**JAPANESE** *	the set $5.95
	* Available Sept. 1, 1959			

UNCONDITIONAL GUARANTEE: Dover Publications stands behind every Listen and Learn record set. If you are dissatisfied with these sets for any reason whatever, return them within 10 days and your money will be refunded in full.

ART HISTORY

STICKS AND STONES, Lewis Mumford. An examination of forces influencing American architecture: the medieval tradition in early New England, the classical influence in Jefferson's time, the Brown Decades, the imperial facade, the machine age, etc. "A truly remarkable book," SAT. REV. OF LITERATURE. 2nd revised edition. 21 illus. xvii + 228pp. 5⅜ x 8.
T202 Paperbound **$1.60**

THE AUTOBIOGRAPHY OF AN IDEA, Louis Sullivan. The architect whom Frank Lloyd Wright called "the master," records the development of the theories that revolutionized America's skyline. 34 full-page plates of Sullivan's finest work. New introduction by R. M. Line. xiv + 335pp. 5⅜ x 8.
T281 Paperbound **$1.85**

THE MATERIALS AND TECHNIQUES OF MEDIEVAL PAINTING, D. V. Thompson. An invaluable study of carriers and grounds, binding media, pigments, metals used in painting, al fresco and al secco techniques, burnishing, etc. used by the medieval masters. Preface by Bernard Berenson. 239pp. 5⅜ x 8.
T327 Paperbound **$1.85**

PRINCIPLES OF ART HISTORY, H. Wölfflin. This remarkably instructive work demonstrates the tremendous change in artistic conception from the 14th to the 18th centuries, by analyzing 164 works by Botticelli, Dürer, Hobbema, Holbein, Hals, Titian, Rembrandt, Vermeer, etc., and pointing out exactly what is meant by "baroque," "classic," "primitive," "picturesque," and other basic terms of art history and criticism. "A remarkable lesson in the art of seeing," SAT. REV. OF LITERATURE. Translated from the 7th German edition. 150 illus. 254pp. 6⅛ x 9¼.
T276 Paperbound **$2.00**

FOUNDATIONS OF MODERN ART, A. Ozenfant. Stimulating discussion of human creativity from paleolithic cave painting to modern painting, architecture, decorative arts. Fully illustrated with works of Gris, Lipchitz, Leger, Picasso, primitive, modern artifacts, architecture, industrial art, much more. 226 illustrations. 368pp. 6⅛ x 9 ,...
T215 Paperbound **$1.95**

HANDICRAFTS, APPLIED ART, ART SOURCES, ETC.

WILD FOWL DECOYS, J. Barber. The standard work on this fascinating branch of folk art, ranging from Indian mud and grass devices to realistic wooden decoys. Discusses styles, types, periods; gives full information on how to make decoys. 140 illustrations (including 14 new plates) show decoys and provide full sets of plans for handicrafters, artists, hunters, and students of folk art. 281pp. 7⅞ x 10¾. Deluxe edition.
T11 Clothbound **$8.50**

METALWORK AND ENAMELLING, H. Maryon. Probably the best book ever written on the subject. Tells everything necessary for the home manufacture of jewelry, rings, ear pendants, bowls, etc. Covers materials, tools, soldering, filigree, setting stones, raising patterns, repoussé work, damascening, niello, cloisonné, polishing, assaying, casting, and dozens of other techniques. The best substitute for apprenticeship to a master metalworker. 363 photos and figures. 374pp. 5½ x 8½.
T183 Clothbound **$7.50**

SHAKER FURNITURE, E. D. and F. Andrews. The most illuminating study of Shaker furniture ever written. Covers chronology, craftsmanship, houses, shops, etc. Includes over 200 photographs of chairs, tables, clocks, beds, benches, etc. "Mr. & Mrs. Andrews know all there is to know about Shaker furniture," Mark Van Doren, NATION. 48 full-page plates. 192pp. Deluxe cloth binding. 7⅞ x 10¾.
T7 Clothbound **$6.00**

PRIMITIVE ART, Franz Boas. A great American anthropologist covers theory, technical virtuosity, styles, symbolism, patterns, etc. of primitive art. The more than 900 illustrations will interest artists, designers, craftworkers. Over 900 illustrations. 376pp. 5⅜ x 8.
T25 Paperbound **$1.95**

ON THE LAWS OF JAPANESE PAINTING, H. Bowie. The best possible substitute for lessons from an oriental master. Treats both spirit and technique; exercises for control of the brush; inks, brushes, colors; use of dots, lines to express whole moods, etc. 220 illus. 132pp. 6⅛ x 9¼.
T30 Paperbound **$1.95**

HANDBOOK OF ORNAMENT, F. S. Meyer. One of the largest collections of copyright-free traditional art: over 3300 line cuts of Greek, Roman, Medieval, Renaissance, Baroque, 18th and 19th century art motifs (tracery, geometric elements, flower and animal motifs, etc.) and decorated objects (chairs, thrones, weapons, vases, jewelry, armor, etc.). Full text. 3300 illustrations. 562pp. 5⅜ x 8.
T302 Paperbound **$2.00**

THREE CLASSICS OF ITALIAN CALLIGRAPHY. Oscar Ogg, ed. Exact reproductions of three famous Renaissance calligraphic works: Arrighi's OPERINA and IL MODO, Tagliente's LO PRESENTE LIBRO, and Palatino's LIBRO NUOVO. More than 200 complete alphabets, thousands of lettered specimens, in Papal Chancery and other beautiful, ornate handwriting. Introduction. 245 plates. 282pp. 6⅛ x 9¼.
T212 Paperbound **$1.95**

THE HISTORY AND TECHNIQUES OF LETTERING, A. Nesbitt. A thorough history of lettering from the ancient Egyptians to the present, and a 65-page course in lettering for artists. Every major development in lettering history is illustrated by a complete alphabet. Fully analyzes such masters as Caslon, Koch, Garamont, Jenson, and many more. 89 alphabets, 165 other specimens. 317pp. 5⅜ x 8.
T427 Paperbound **$2.00**

LETTERING AND ALPHABETS, J. A. Cavanagh. An unabridged reissue of "Lettering," containing the full discussion, analysis, illustration of 89 basic hand lettering tyles based on Caslon, Bodoni, Gothic, many other types. Hundreds of technical hints on construction, strokes, pens, brushes, etc. 89 alphabets, 72 lettered specimens, which may be reproduced permission-free. 121pp. 9¾ x 8. T53 Paperbound **$1.25**

THE HUMAN FIGURÉ IN MOTION, Eadweard Muybridge. The largest collection in print of Muybridge's famous high-speed action photos. 4789 photographs in more than 500 action-strip-sequences (at shutter speeds up to 1/6000th of a second) illustrate men, women, children—mostly undraped—performing such actions as walking, running, getting up, lying down, carrying objects, throwing, etc. "An unparalleled dictionary of action for all artists," AMERICAN ARTIST. 390 full-page plates, with 4789 photographs. Heavy glossy stock, reinforced binding with headbands. 7⅞ x 10¾. T204 Clothbound **$10.00**

ANIMALS IN MOTION, Eadweard Muybridge. The largest collection of animal action photos in print. 34 different animals (horses, mules, oxen, goats, camels, pigs, cats, lions, gnus, deer, monkeys, eagles—and 22 others) in 132 characteristic actions. All 3919 photographs are taken in series at speeds up to 1/1600th of a second, offering artists, biologists, cartoonists a remarkable opportunity to see exactly how an ostrich's head bobs when running, how a lion puts his foot down, how an elephant's knee bends, how a bird flaps his wings, thousands of other hard-to-catch details. "A really marvelous series of plates," NATURE. 380 full-pages of plates. Heavy glossy stock, reinforced binding with headbands. 7⅞ x 10¾. T203 Clothbound **$10.00**

THE BOOK OF SIGNS, R. Koch. 493 symbols—crosses, monograms, astrological, biological symbols, runes, etc.—from ancient manuscripts, cathedrals, coins, catacombs, pottery. May be reproduced permission-free. 493 illustrations by Fritz Kredel. 104pp. 6⅛ x 9¼. T162 Paperbound **$1.00**

A HANDBOOK OF EARLY ADVERTISING ART, C. P. Hornung. The largest collection of copyright-free early advertising art ever compiled. Vol. I: 2,000 illustrations of animals, old automobiles, buildings, allegorical figures, fire engines, Indians, ships, trains, more than 33 other categories! Vol II: Over 4,000 typographical specimens; 600 Roman, Gothic, Barnum, Old English faces; 630 ornamental type faces; hundreds of scrolls, initials, flourishes, etc. "A remarkable collection," PRINTERS' INK.

Vol. I: Pictorial Volume. Over 2000 illustrations. 256pp. 9 x 12. T122 Clothbound **$10.00**

Vol. II: Typographical Volume. Over 4000 specimens. 319pp. 9 x 12. T123 Clothbound **$10.00**
Two volume set, Clothbound, only **$18.50**

DESIGN FOR ARTISTS AND CRAFTSMEN, L. Wolchonok. The most thorough course on the creation of art motifs and designs. Shows you step-by-step, with hundreds of examples and 113 detailed exercises, how to create original designs from geometric patterns, plants, birds, animals, humans, and man-made objects. "A great contribution to the field of design and crafts," N. Y. SOCIETY OF CRAFTSMEN. More than 1300 entirely new illustrations. xv + 207pp. 7⅞ x 10¾. T274 Clothbound **$4.95**

HANDBOOK OF DESIGNS AND DEVICES, C. P. Hornung. A remarkable working collection of 1836 basic designs and variations, all copyright-free. Variations of circle, line, cross, diamond, swastika, star, scroll, shield, many more. Notes on symbolism. "A necessity to every designer who would be original without having to labor heavily," ARTIST and ADVERTISER. 204 plates. 240pp. 5⅜ x 8.

T125 Paperbound **$1.90**

THE UNIVERSAL PENMAN, George Bickham. Exact reproduction of beautiful 18th century book of handwriting. 22 complete alphabets in finest English roundhand, other scripts, over 2000 elaborate flourishes, 122 calligraphic illustrations, etc. Material is copyright-free. "An essential part of any art library, and a book of permanent value," AMERICAN ARTIST. 212 plates. 224pp. 9 x 13¾. T20 Clothbound **$10.00**

AN ATLAS OF ANATOMY FOR ARTISTS, F. Schider. This standard work contains 189 full-page plates, more than 647 illustrations of all aspects of the human skeleton, musculature, cutaway portions of the body, each part of the anatomy, hand forms, eyelids, breasts, location of muscles under the flesh, etc. 59 plates illustrate how Michelangelo, da Vinci, Goya, 15 others, drew human anatomy. New 3rd edition enlarged by 52 new illustrations by Cloquet, Barcsay. "The standard reference tool," AMERICAN LIBRARY ASSOCIATION. "Excellent," AMERICAN ARTIST. 189 plates, 647 illustrations. xxvi + 192pp. 7⅞ x 10⅝. T241 Clothbound **$6.00**

AN ATLAS OF ANIMAL ANATOMY FOR ARTISTS, W. Ellenberger, H. Baum, H. Dittrich. The largest, richest animal anatomy for artists in English. Form, musculature, tendons, bone structure, expression, detailed cross sections of head, other features, of the horse, lion, dog, cat, deer, seal, kangaroo, cow, bull, goat, monkey, hare, many other animals. "Highly recommended," DESIGN. Second, revised, enlarged edition with new plates from Cuvier, Stubbs, etc. 288 illustrations. 153pp. 11⅜ x 9. T82 Clothbound **$6.00**

ANIMAL DRAWING: ANATOMY AND ACTION FOR ARTISTS, C. R. Knight. 158 studies, with full accompanying text, of such animals as the gorilla, bear, bison, dromedary, camel, vulture, pelican, iguana, shark, etc., by one of the greatest modern masters of animal drawing. Innumerable tips on how to get life expression into your work. "An excellent reference work,' SAN FRANCISCO CHRONICLE. 158 illustrations. 156pp. 10½ x 8½. T426 Paperbound **$2.00**

DOVER BOOKS

THE CRAFTSMAN'S HANDBOOK, Cennino Cennini. The finest English translation of IL LIBRO DELL' ARTE, the 15th century introduction to art technique that is both a mirror of Quatrocento life and a source of many useful but ·nearly forgotten facets of the painter's art. 4 illustrations. xxvii + 142pp. D. V. Thompson, translator. 6⅛ x 9¼.   T54 Paperbound **$1.50**

THE BROWN DECADES, Lewis Mumford. A picture of the "buried renaissance" of the post-Civil War period, and the founding of modern architecture (Sullivan, Richardson, Root, Roebling), landscape development (Marsh, Olmstead, Eliot), and the graphic arts (Homer, Eakins, Ryder). 2nd revised, enlarged edition. Bibliography. 12 illustrations. xiv + 266 pp. 5⅜ x 8.   T200 Paperbound **$1.65**

STIEGEL GLASS, F. W. Hunter. The story of the most highly esteemed early American glassware, fully illustrated. How a German adventurer, "Baron" Stiegel, founded a glass empire; detailed accounts of individual glasswork. "This pioneer work is reprinted in an edition even more beautiful than the original," ANTIQUES DEALER. New introduction by Helen McKearin. 171 illustrations, 12 in full color. xxii + 338pp. 7⅞ x 10¾.
    T128 Clothbound **$10.00**

THE HUMAN FIGURE, J. H. Vanderpoel. Not just a picture book, but a complete course by a famous figure artist. Extensive text, illustrated by 430 pencil and charcoal drawings of both male and female anatomy. 2nd enlarged edition. Foreword. 430 illus. 143pp. 6⅛ x 9¼.
    T432 Paperbound **$1.45**

PINE FURNITURE OF EARLY NEW ENGLAND, R. H. Kettell. Over 400 illustrations, over 50 working drawings of early New England chairs, benches, beds cupboards, mirrors, shelves, tables, other furniture esteemed for simple beauty and character. "Rich store of illustrations . . . emphasizes the individuality and varied design," ANTIQUES. 413 illustrations, 55 working drawings. 475pp. 8 x 10¾.   T145 Clothbound **$10.00**

BASIC BOOKBINDING, A. W. Lewis. Enables both beginners and experts to rebind old books or bind paperbacks in hard covers. Treats materials, tools; gives step-by-step instruction in how to collate a book, sew it, back it, make boards, etc. 261 illus. Appendices. 155pp. 5⅜ x 8.   T169 Paperbound **$1.35**

DESIGN MOTIFS OF ANCIENT MEXICO, J. Enciso. Nearly 90% of these 766 superb designs from Aztec, Olmec, Totonac, Maya, and Toltec origins are unobtainable elsewhere! Contains plumed serpents, wind gods, animals, demons, dancers, monsters, etc. Excellent applied design source. Originally $17.50. 766 illustrations, thousands of motifs. 192pp. 6⅛ x 9¼.
    T84 Paperbound **$1.85**

AFRICAN SCULPTURE, Ladislas Segy. 163 full-page plates illustrating masks, fertility figures, ceremonial objects, etc., of 50 West and Central African tribes—95% never before illustrated. 34-page introduction to African sculpture. "Mr. Segy is one of its top authorities," NEW YORKER. 164 full-page photographic plates. Introduction. Bibliography. 244pp. 6⅛ x 9¼.
    T396 Paperbound **$2.00**

THE PROCESSES OF GRAPHIC REPRODUCTION IN PRINTING, H. Curwen. A thorough and practical survey of wood, linoleum, and rubber engraving; copper engraving; drypoint, mezzotint, etching, aquatint, steel engraving, die sinking, stencilling, lithography (extensively); photographic reproduction utilizing line, continuous tone, photoengravure, collotype; every other process in general use. Note on color reproduction. Section on bookbinding. Over 200 illustrations, 25 in color. 143pp. 5½ x 8½.   T512 Clothbound **$4.00**

CALLIGRAPHY, J. G. Schwandner. First reprinting in 200 years of this legendary book of beautiful handwriting. Over 300 ornamental initials, 12 complete calligraphic alphabets, over 150 ornate frames and panels, 75 calligraphic pictures of cherubs, stags, lions, etc., thousands of flourishes, scrolls, etc., by the greatest 18th century masters. All material can be copied or adapted without permission. Historical introduction. 158 full-page plates. 368pp. 9 x 13.   T475 Clothbound **$10.00**

* * *

A DIDEROT PICTORIAL ENCYCLOPEDIA OF TRADES AND INDUSTRY, Manufacturing and the Technical Arts in Plates Selected from "L'Encyclopédie ou Dictionnaire Raisonné des Sciences, des Arts, et des Métiers," of Denis Diderot, edited with text by C. Gillispie. Over 2000 illustrations on 485 full-page plates. Magnificent 18th century engravings of men, women, and children working at such trades as milling flour, cheesemaking, charcoal burning, mining, silverplating, shoeing horses, making fine glass, printing, hundreds more, showing details of machinery, different steps. in sequence, etc. A remarkable art work, but also the largest collection of working figures in print, copyright‑free, for art directors, designers, etc. Two vols. 920pp. 9 x 12. Heavy library cloth.   T421 Two volume set **$18.50**

* * *

SILK SCREEN TECHNIQUES, J. Biegeleisen, M. Cohn. A practical step-by-step home course in one of the most versatile, least expensive graphic arts processes. How to build an inexpensive silk screen, prepare stencils, print, achieve special textures, use color, etc. Every step explained, diagrammed. 149 illustrations, 8 in color. 201pp. 6⅛ x 9¼.
    T433 Paperbound **$1.45**

PUZZLES, GAMES, AND ENTERTAINMENTS

MATHEMATICS, MAGIC AND MYSTERY, Martin Gardner. Astonishing feats of mind reading, mystifying "magic" tricks, are often based on mathematical principles anyone can learn. This book shows you how to perform scores of tricks with cards, dice, coins, knots, numbers, etc., by using simple principles from set theory, theory of numbers, topology, other areas of mathematics, fascinating in themselves. No special knowledge required. 135 illus. 186pp. 5⅜ x 8. T335 Paperbound **$1.00**

MATHEMATICAL PUZZLES FOR BEGINNERS AND ENTHUSIASTS, G. Mott-Smoth. Test your problem-solving techniques and powers of inference on 188 challenging, amusing puzzles based on algebra, dissection of plane figures, permutations, probabilities, etc. Appendix of primes, square roots, etc. 135 illus. 2nd revised edition. 248pp. 5⅜ x 8.
T198 Paperbound **$1.00**

LEARN CHESS FROM THE MASTERS, F. Reinfeld. Play 10 games against Marshall, Bronstein, Najdorf, other masters, and grade yourself on each move. Detailed annotations reveal principles of play, strategy, etc. as you proceed. An excellent way to get a real insight into the game. Formerly titled, "Chess by Yourself." 91 diagrams. vii + 144pp. 5⅜ x 8.
T362 Paperbound **$1.00**

REINFELD ON THE END GAME IN CHESS, F. Reinfeld. 62 end games of Alekhine, Tarrasch, Morphy, other masters, are carefully analyzed with emphasis on transition from middle game to end play. Tempo moves, queen endings, weak squares, other basic principles clearly illustrated. Excellent for understanding why some moves are weak or incorrect, how to avoid errors. Formerly titled, "Practical End-game Play." 62 diagrams. vi + 177pp. 5⅜ x 8.
T417 Paperbound **$1.25**

101 PUZZLES IN THOUGHT AND LOGIC, C. R. Wylie, Jr. Brand new puzzles you need no special knowledge to solve! Each one is a gem of ingenuity that will really challenge your problem-solving technique. Introduction with simplified explanation of scienti ̄c puzzle solving. 128pp. 5⅜ x 8. T167 Paperbound **$1.00**

THE COMPLETE NONSENSE OF EDWARD LEAR. The only complete edition of this master of gentle madness at a popular price. The Dong with the Luminous Nose, The Jumblies, The Owl and the Pussycat, hundreds of other bits of wonderful nonsense. 214 limericks, 3 sets of Nonsense Botany, 5 Nonsense Alphabets, 546 fantastic drawings, much more. 320pp. 5⅜ x 8. T167 Paperbound **$1.00**

28 SCIENCE FICTION STORIES OF H. G. WELLS. Two complete novels, "Men Like Gods" and "Star Begotten," plus 26 short stories by the master science-fiction writer of all time. Stories of space, time, future adventure that are among the all-time classics of science fiction. 928pp. 5⅜ x 8. T265 Clothbound **$3.95**

SEVEN SCIENCE FICTION NOVELS, H. G. Wells. Unabridged texts of "The Time Machine," "The Island of Dr. Moreau," "First Men in the Moon," "The Invisible Man," "The War of the Worlds," "The Food of the Gods," "In the Days of the Comet." "One will have to go far to match this for entertainment, excitement, and sheer pleasure," N. Y. TIMES. 1015pp. 5⅜ x 8. T264 Clothbound **$3.95**

MATHEMAGIC, MAGIC PUZZLES, AND GAMES WITH NUMBERS, R. V. Heath. More than 60 new puzzles and stunts based on number properties: multiplying large numbers mentally, finding the date of any day in the year, etc. Edited by J. S. Meyer. 76 illus. 129pp. 5⅜ x 8.
T110 Paperbound **$1.00**

FIVE ADVENTURE NOVELS OF H. RIDER HAGGARD. The master story-teller's five best tales of mystery and adventure set against authentic African backgrounds: "She," "King Solomon's Mines," "Allan Quatermain," "Allan's Wife," "Maiwa's Revenge." 821pp. 5⅜ x 8.
T108 Clothbound **$3.95**

WIN AT CHECKERS, M. Hopper. (Formerly "Checkers.") The former World's Unrestricted Checker Champion gives you valuable lessons in openings, traps, end games, ways to draw when you are behind, etc. More than 100 questions and answers anticipate your problems. Appendix. 75 problems diagrammed, solved. 79 figures. xi + 107pp. 5⅜ x 8.
T363 Paperbound **$1.00**

CRYPTOGRAPHY, L. D. Smith. Excellent introductory work on ciphers and their solution, history of secret writing, techniques, etc. Appendices on Japanese methods, the Baconian cipher, frequency tables. Bibliography. Over 150 problems, solutions. 160pp. 5⅜ x 8.
T247 Paperbound **$1.00**

CRYPTANALYSIS, H. F. Gaines. (Formerly, "Elementary Cryptanalysis.") The best book available on cryptograms and how to solve them. Contains all major techniques: substitution, transposition, mixed alphabets, multafid, Kasiski and Vignere methods, etc. Word frequency appendix. 167 problems, solutions. 173 figures. 236pp. 5⅜ x 8. T97 Paperbound **$1.95**

FLATLAND, E. A. Abbot. The science-fiction classic of life in a 2-dimensional world that is considered a first-rate introduction to relativity and hyperspace, as well as a scathing satire on society, politics and religion. 7th edition. 16 illus. 128pp. 5⅜ x 8.
T1 Paperbound **$1.00**

DOVER BOOKS

HOW TO FORCE CHECKMATE, F. Reinfeld. (Formerly "Challenge to Chessplayers.") No board needed to sharpen your checkmate skill on 300 checkmate situations. Learn to plan up to 3 moves ahead and play a superior end game. 300 situations diagrammed; notes and full solutions. 111pp. 5⅜ x 8. T439 Paperbound **$1.25**

MORPHY'S GAMES OF CHESS, P. W. Sergeant, ed. Play forcefully by following the techniques used by one of.the greatest chess champions. 300 of Morphy's games carefully annotated to reveal principles. Bibliography. New introduction by F. Reinfeld. 235 diagrams. x + 352pp. 5⅜ x 8. T386 Paperbound **$1.75**

MATHEMATICAL RECREATIONS, M. Kraitchik. Hundreds of unusual mathematical puzzlers and odd bypaths of math, elementary and advanced. Greek, Medieval, Arabic, Hindu problems; figurate numbers, Fermat numbers, primes; magic, Euler, Latin squares; fairy chess, latruncles, reversi, jinx, ruma, tetrachrome other positional and permutational games. Rigorous solutions. Revised second edition. 181 illus. 330pp. 5⅜ x 8. T163 Paperbound **$1.75**

MATHEMATICAL EXCURSIONS, H. A. Merrill. Revealing stimulating insights into elementary math, not usually taught in school. 90 problems demonstrate Russian peasant multiplication, memory systems for pi, magic squares, dyadic systems, division by inspection, many more. Solutions to difficult problems. 50 illus. 5⅜ x 8. T350 Paperbound **$1.00**

MAGIC TRICKS & CARD TRICKS, W. Jonson. Best introduction to tricks with coins, bills, eggs, ribbons, slates, cards, easily performed without elaborate equipment. Professional routines, tips on presentation, misdirection, etc. Two books bound as one: 52 tricks with cards, 37 tricks with common objects. 106 figures. 224pp. 5⅜ x 8. T909 Paperbound **$1.00**

MATHEMATICAL PUZZLES OF SAM LOYD, selected and edited by **M. Gardner.** 177 most ingenious mathematical puzzles of America's greatest puzzle originator, based on arithmetic, algebra, game theory, dissection, route tracing, operations research, probability, etc. 120 drawings, diagrams. Solutions. 187pp. 5⅜ x 8. T498 Paperbound **$1.00**

THE ART OF CHESS, J. Mason. The most famous general study of chess ever written. More than 90 openings, middle game, end game, how to attack, sacrifice, defend, exchange, form general strategy. Supplement on "How Do You Play Chess?" by F. Reinfeld. 448 diagrams. 356pp. 5⅜ x 8. T463 Paperbound **$1.85**

HYPERMODERN CHESS as Developed in the Games of its Greatest Exponent, ARON NIMZOVICH, F. Reinfeld, ed. Learn how the game's greatest innovator defeated Alekhine, Lasker, and many others; and use these methods in your own game. 180 diagrams. 228pp. 5⅜ x 8. T448 Paperbound **$1.35**

A TREASURY OF CHESS LORE, F. Reinfeld, ed. Hundreds of fascinating stories by and about the masters, accounts of tournaments and famous games, aphorisms, word portraits, little known incidents, photographs, etc., that will delight the chess enthusiast, captivate the beginner. 49 photographs (14 full-page plates), 12 diagrams. 315pp. 5⅜ x 8. T458 Paperbound **$1.75**

A NONSENSE ANTHOLOGY, collected by **Carolyn Wells.** 245 of the best nonsense verses ever written: nonsense puns, absurd arguments, mock epics, nonsense ballads, "sick" verses, dog-Latin verses, French nonsense verses, limericks. Lear, Carroll, Belloc, Burgess, nearly 100 other writers. Introduction by Carolyn Wells. 3 indices: Title, Author, First Lines. xxxiii + 279pp. 5⅜ x 8. T499 Paperbound **$1.25**

SYMBOLIC LOGIC and THE GAME OF LOGIC, Lewis Carroll. Two delightful puzzle books by the author of "Alice," bound as one. Both works concern the symbolic representation of traditional logic and together contain more than 500 ingenious, amusing and instructive syllogistic puzzlers. Total of 326pp. 5⅜ x 8. T492 Paperbound **$1.50**

PILLOW PROBLEMS and A TANGLED TALE, Lewis Carroll. Two of Carroll's rare puzzle works bound as one. "Pillow Problems" contain 72 original math puzzles. The puzzles in "A Tangled Tale" are given in delightful story form. Total of 291pp. 5⅜ x 8. T493 Paperbound **$1.50**

PECK'S BAD BOY AND HIS PA, G. W. Peck. Both volumes of one of the most widely read of all American humor books. A classic of American folk humor, also invaluable as a portrait of an age. 100 original illustrations. Introduction by E. Bleiler. 347pp. 5⅜ x 8. T497 Paperbound **$1.35**

Dover publishes books on art, music, philosophy, literature, languages, history, social sciences, psychology, handcrafts, orientalia, puzzles and entertainments, chess, pets and gardens, books explaining science, intermediate and higher mathematics mathematical physics, engineering, biological sciences, earth sciences, classics of science, etc. Write to:

Dept. catrr.
Dover Publications, Inc.
180 Varick Street, N. Y. 14, N. Y.